Information Visualization

ACM Press Books

This book is published as part of ACM Press Books – a collaboration between the Association for Computing Machinery (ACM) and Addison Wesley Longman Limited. ACM is the oldest and largest educational and scientific society in the information technology field. Through its high-quality publications and services, ACM is a major force in advancing the skills and knowledge of IT professionals throughout the world. For further information about ACM, contact:

ACM Member Services
1515 Broadway, 17th Floor
New York, NY 10036-5701
Phone: 1-212-626-0500
Fax: 1-212-944-1318
E-mail: acmhelp@acm.org
URL: http://www.acm.org/

ACM European Service Center
108 Cowley Road
Oxford OX4 1JF
United Kingdom
Phone: +44-1865-382388
Fax: +44-1865-381388
E-mail: acm_europe@acm.org
URL: http://www.acm.org/

Information Visualization

Robert Spence

 Addison-Wesley

An imprint of **Pearson Education**

Harlow, England · London · New York · Reading, Massachusetts · San Francisco
Toronto · Don Mills, Ontario · Sydney · Tokyo · Singapore · Hong Kong · Seoul
Taipei · Cape Town · Madrid · Mexico City · Amsterdam · Munich · Paris · Milan

Pearson Education Limited
Edinburgh Gate
Harlow
Essex CM20 2JE
England

and Associated Companies throughout the world

Visit us on the World Wide Web at:
www.pearsoneduc.com

ISBN 0-201-59626-1

British Library Cataloguing-in-Publication Data
A catalogue record for this book can be obtained from the British Library

Library of Congress Cataloging-in-Publication Data
A catalog record for this book can be obtained from the Library of Congress

10 9 8 7 6 5 4 3 2
05 04 03 02 01

Text design by Design Deluxe, Bath
Typeset in Caslon 224 by 30
Printed and bound by Rotolito Lombarda, Italy

To Kathy

A Companion Web Site

accompanies *Information Visualization*

by Robert Spence

Visit the *Information Visualization* Companion Web Site at
www.booksites.net/spence

Here you will find valuable teaching and learning material including:

For Lecturers:
- Suggestions and guidance on how to use the book to accompany your course.
- Sample solutions to the exercises provided in the Student area of the web site.
- OHPs to aid teaching some of the material.
- Links to useful resources on the web.

For Students:
- Exercises to accompany the text.
- Examples of dynamic information visualization in action.
- Links to resources on the web.

Contents

Chapter 3   Interpretation of Quantitative Data   33

Chapter 4   Representation   52

Chapter 5   Dynamic Exploration   70

Chapter 6 Internal Models, their Formation and Interpretation   92

Chapter 10   Document Visualization   175

Trademark Notice

The following are trademarks or registered trademarks of their respective companies.

IBM is a registered trademark of International Business Machines Corporation (IBM).

The letters ICI are a trademark of the ICI Group of companies.

Netmap is a registered trademark of ALTA Europe Ltd.

Table Lens, Cone Tree, Perspective Wall, Document Lens and Hyperbolic Tree are trademarks of Inxight Software, Inc.

Preface

You are the owner of some numerical data which, you feel, is hiding some fundamental relation which could be exploited to your advantage, perhaps for business or merely for pleasure. You then glance at some visual presentation of that data and exclaim 'Ah ha! – *now* I understand'. That is what information visualization is about. It is the process of forming a mental model of data, thereby gaining insight into that data.

Although that sudden acquisition of insight might on occasion be followed by a statistical investigation, that is not my concern here. Rather, I concentrate on the acquisition of insight through the identification of patterns and other features of a display. That insight could lead to the identification of a criminal, to a profitable financial investment, to the identification of a source of pollution or to the discovery of the house of your dreams in the portfolio of an estate agent. On a less serious note it could form part of a casual and entertaining perusal of last season's baseball statistics. All these examples occur in the book's illustrations, of which there are many.

It is important to distinguish information visualization, which is the subject of this book, from 'scientific visualization', which is not. In scientific visualization what is seen primarily relates to, and represents visually, something 'physical'. Thus, the flow of water in a pipe, the nature of the weather in a mountainous area and the stresses in a girder are usually – and usefully – displayed directly superimposed on, or at least close to, a realistic representation of the physical thing. By contrast, information visualization tends to deal with abstract quantities such as baseball scores, connections between known criminals, fluctuating exchange rates and electrical voltages. These quantities relate to real things, to be sure, but there is little to be gained, for example, by displaying pictures of dollar bills and sterling notes when trying to communicate fast changing exchange rates to a currency dealer. Inevitably there is some overlap between these two forms of visualization, but I concentrate here on the problem of enhancing a human being's acquisition of insight into abstract data.

A glance at the two hundred or so references I've cited will hint at one significant fact which is directly related to the *raison d'être* of the book: most of them carry a date between 1990 and 2000 AD. What happened during the last decade? The answer is simple: the emergence of inexpensive powerful computers, high-quality graphics, cheap memory and responsive interaction stimulated the invention of an exciting new class of visualization tools. Earlier studies of data visualization mainly had the professional scientist as the target customer, concentrated on the examination of static presentations of data and were closely associated with statistical analysis. By contrast, and as a result of technological progress, the benefits of information visualization are now available to a much wider range of customers ranging from supermarket managers to fraud investigators. Now, dynamic as well as static presentations of data can be interpreted, and interaction brings the considerable power of rearrangement to the user, who can now ask 'what if?' questions and receive immediate answers. A shift in emphasis away from statistical studies and towards the formation of a mental model has brought with it a realization of the wide range of potential applications for information visualization; illustrative examples range from electronic commerce to the anthropomorphic representation of people surfing the World Wide Web.

Information visualization is characterized by so many beautiful images that there is a danger of adopting a 'Gee Whiz' approach to its presentation. I try, I hope successfully, to avoid this danger, but I also avoid any temptation to write an encyclopedia on the subject. I have, in fact, had two objectives in mind. I have aimed for a scholarly text – by striving for appropriate rigour and structure – while trying to provide a readable text suited to a wide spectrum of readers ranging from the CEO to the software engineer. If 'dip-in-able' is an English word – and even if it isn't – I would say that it describes another objective, since I have tried to make it possible for the interested reader to open the book almost anywhere and dip in to learn about a new visualization technique.

My original plan was to include a concluding chapter dedicated to a review of general theories of information visualization, theories that would encompass many of the 'point solutions' illustrated by the book's many examples. On reflection I realized that whereas the 'nineties saw the invention of these powerful 'point solutions' it will take the next decade (the 'noughties'?) for general theories to be established with some confidence.

Many academics have expressed their intention to adopt the book in university and college courses. While that delights me, I should warn them of the difficulty of setting examination papers that do something more exciting and helpful than testing memory; specifically, a 30-minute question is not the ideal way in which to evaluate a student's ability to *design* visualization tools. For this reason my colleagues and I are creating a compilation of exercises that may be found useful by teachers of information visualization. I'd be very happy for those teachers to contact me.

Robert Spence
Imperial College
1 May 2000

Acknowledgements

I've derived a great deal of excitement and pleasure from researching the field of information visualization, and that is due in very large measure to those colleagues I've been privileged to work with. They go back as far as 1968, when Tony Drew helped me to explore information visualization (though it wasn't called that at the time!) in the context of interactive-graphic circuit design. In 1971 there began a collaboration with Mark Apperley that has been very productive and is still active. Soon afterwards Paul Rankin was instrumental, in the early 'eighties, in ensuring that a number of visualization techniques were brought to market via the MINNIE system for computer aided design, and around a decade later we were joined by Lynne Colgan to devise visualization tools for another novel system, called CoCo, which facilitated the human observation and guidance of automated engineering design. At the same time Maureen Parr helped me to improve my understanding of multidimensional icons.

My research into information visualization intensified around 1993 with our invention of the Attribute Explorer, initially with help from David Williams and Ravinder Bhogal. It was at this time that I was fortunate enough to be joined by Lisa Tweedie, for there then began a very productive collaboration which led, among other things, to the Influence Explorer, the Prosection Matrix and many other concepts relevant to information visualization. Valuable contributions were made at that time by Huw Dawkes, Hua Su, Zahid Malik, Andrew Smith and John Nelder. Two very successful undergraduate projects introduced me to Kevin Lam and Rick Boardman, and I am fortunate that Rick has returned to continue our collaboration. A more recent collaboration with Oscar de Bruijn is already proving extremely fruitful. To all these very good friends I am immensely grateful.

Encouragement is a much valued commodity, and I have received this in good measure from Ken Chakhawahta and Patrick Purcell. Help at various stages was kindly supplied by many people around the world: Marti Hearst of Berkeley, Antony Unwin of Augsberg, Ken Fishkin of Xerox PARC, Daniel Keim from Germany, students and staff of the Center for Human–Computer Systems at the Technical University of Eindhoven, Harald Noordhoek from The Netherlands, Lars Holmquist and Staffan Bjork from Sweden, Chris Ahlberg, also from Sweden, David Snoken of ALTA Europe, David McIlroy from Belgium, Murray Shanahan and Andrew Smith, both from Imperial College, Ron MacNeill of MIT, David Lantrip, James Miller, Bob Waddington, Matthew Chalmers, Mei Chuah, Kent Wittenburg, Mark Apperley, Mark Goosman, Alan MacEachren, Neil Mothew, Steve Roth, Xia Lin, Dick Bolt, Michael Friendly, George Grinstein, Daniel Keim, John Peters and Colin Ware. My warmest thanks to all of them. Much closer (thankfully) are my colleagues in the Departmental Library, namely Ellen, Don and Gavin, and Kay Hancox who can persuade my computer to do terribly clever things. In the production of the book it was a pleasure to work with Keith Mansfield, Richard Lamprecht and Magda Robson of Pearson Education.

Over many years I have also been fortunate enough to meet regularly with those who might be called the 'household names' of information visualization: Stu Card, Ben Shneiderman, Steve Eick, Ramana Rao and many others, all of whom have very kindly allowed me to use some of the images illustrating their work. It is also a pleasure to acknowledge that I derived considerable stimulation from a book, *Readings in Information Visualization*, authored by Stu Card, Jock Mackinlay and Ben Shneiderman, a truly scholarly exposition commenting on a selection of around forty seminal papers in the field. Those wishing to dig deeper by consulting papers that have helped to shape the future of information visualization are strongly recommended to acquire that book.

In the pages that follow I comment extensively about the importance of context: one that has stimulated and supported me during the preparation of this book is the person to whom it is dedicated with love and appreciation.

The author and the publishers are grateful to the following for permission to reproduce copyright material:

Figs 1.1, 7.14, 8.1 London Underground Map designed by H. F. Stingemore (1927), © London Transport and 8.2 London Underground Map designed by Harry Beck (1933), © London Transport. Reproduced by kind permission of London Transport Museum; Figs 1.4 and 1.6 from Tufte, E. (1983) *The Visual Display of Quantitative Information* reproduced by permission of Graphics Press, Cheshire, Connecticut; Fig. 1.7 reproduced by permission of Ken Garland; Figs 1.8 and 1.9 from Maclean, N. (1992) *Young Men and Fire*, reproduced by permission of The University of Chicago Press; Fig. 2.1 reproduced by permission of Bob Waddington; Figs 2.2, 8.31, 8.32, 8.33 and 8.34 reproduced by permission of Inxight Software, Inc; Figs 2.13, 2.14 and 2.15 from Chuah, M. C. et al. (1995) SDM: *Selective Dynamic Manipulation of Visualizations* (UIST'95, pp.61–70), reproduced by kind permission of the author and Association for Computing Machinery, Inc.; Fig. 2.17 reproduced by permission of Matthew Chalmers; Fig 3.10 from Cleveland, W.S. (1985) *The Elements of Graphing Data* (Wadsworth Advanced Book Program, A Division of Wadsworth, Inc.) copyright © 1985 Bell Telephone Laboratories, Inc., reproduced by permission of Kluwer Academic Publishers; Fig. 3.19 a and b images produced by IDL (Interactive Data Language) and reproduced by permission; Fig. 3.22 reproduced by permission from the IBM Corp.; Fig. 4.6 from Smith D. (1999) *The State of the World Atlas*, 6th edition, published by Penguin and reproduced with permission from Myriad Editions Limited; Fig. 4.14 from Eick, S. G., Staffen, J. L. and Sumner, E. E. (1992) 'Seesoft – A Tool Visualizing Line Oriented Software Statistics', *IEEE Transactions on Software Engineering*, 18, 11, reproduced by permission of IEEE © 1992 IEEE; Fig. 4.15 reproduced by permission of Georges Grinstein; Fig. 4.16 StarCursor Design © Philips Electronics N.V. 1998, reproduced by permission; Figs 4.20 and 4.21 reproduced by permission of Alan MacEachren; Figs 5.2 and 5.5 reproduced by permission of Spotfire AB; Fig. 6.14 reproduced by permission of Philips Media; Fig. 6.20 reproduced by permission of The MIT Media Laboratory; Fig 7.5 reproduced by permission of Colin Ware; Figs 7.18 and 7.19 from Mitta, D. A. (1990) 'A Fisheye Presentation Strategy: Aircraft Maintenance Data' in Daiper *et al.* (eds) *Human–Computer Interaction – INTERACT '90* North-Holland/IFIP, pp.875–880, reproduced by permission of IFIP; Fig, 7.21 from *Frames* February 1992, reproduced by permission of Ron MacNeil; Figs 7.25 and 7.26 reproduced by permission from GTE Laboratories, Inc; Fig. 8.3 from Arnold, C. J. (1997) *An Archaeology of the Early Anglo-Saxon Kingdoms* (pub Routledge), reproduced by permission of ITPS Ltd; Figs 8.7 and 8.8 from Becker, R. A., Eick, S. G. and Wilks, A. R. (1995) 'Visualizing Network Data', *IEEE Transactions on Visualization and Computer Graphics*, 1 (1 March), reproduced by permission of IEEE © 1995 IEEE; Fig. 8.10 from Eick, S. G. and Wills, G. J. (1993) 'Navigating Large Networks with Hierarchies', *Proceeding of IEEE Visualization '93 Conference*, reproduced by permission of IEEE © 1993 IEEE; Figs 8.13, 8.14, 8.15 and 8.16 reproduced by permission of ALTA Europe Ltd; Fig. 8.17 reproduced by permission of Daisy Analysis; Fig 8.25 reproduced by permission of Xerox Corporation; Fig. 9.21 from Stasko, J. T. and Domingue, J. M. (1998) *Software Visualization: Programming as a Multimedia*, reproduced by permission of The MIT Press © 1998 Massachusetts Institute of Technology; Figs 10.3 and 10.4 reproduced by permission of Marti Hearst; Figs 10.8 and 10.9 from the Themescape 2.0 product reproduced by permission of Cartia, Inc., Bellevue, WA, USA; Fig. 10.10 from Rennison, E. (1994) *Galaxy of News: An Approach to Visualizing and Understanding* (UIST'94, pp.3–12), reproduced by permission of Association for Computing Machinery, Inc.; Fig. 10.11 reproduced by permission of Xia Lin.

Every effort has been made to trace copyright material. However, in the event that any have been overlooked, the Publishers will make the necessary amendment at the earliest opportunity.

CHAPTER 1

Issues

1.1 What is visualization?

Terminology is a problem in many fields of study. Familiar terms are often used very loosely, even though important concepts are being addressed. Does it matter? Yes, it does, because many useful insights can occur if we know precisely what we're talking about.

'Visualization' is a case in point. Is it something a computer does, as implied by a great many texts, or an activity carried out by a human being? Let's reach for one or two dictionaries.[1]

> *visualize: (vb) to form a mental image or vision of . . .*
> *visualize: (vb) to imagine or remember as if actually seeing.*

Immediately we realize that visualization is an activity which a human being engages in, and that it is a *cognitive* activity (Ware, 2000; MacEachren, 1995): in other words, it goes on in the mind. Indeed, it results in something rather ephemeral (which we later call a mental model or internal model), something that cannot be printed out on paper or viewed through a microscope. The result is, as we say, *internal* to the human being. The potential value of visualization – that of gaining insight and understanding – follows from these definitions but so also, in view of the cognitive nature of visualization does the difficulty of its study.

---

[1] The American Heritage and Concise Oxford dictionaries.

Intentionally, no mention has yet been made of the computer, of which the above definitions are independent (Spence, 1996). Indeed, they will remain so, though we shall certainly investigate how the computer can facilitate the visualization process with what we shall call visualization tools.

1.2 Information visualization

There are many situations in which data is available, sometimes in very large quantities, and where some human insight into that data is required. Two simple examples will suffice for the moment. One is associated with the familiar London Underground railway map (Figure 1.1). Sight of the map results in the viewer forming in his or her mind some understanding – though not a completely memorized image – of the underground railway routes and their regular and interchange stations. Typically, attention will focus on the planned journey, and hence on the intended departure and destination stations and a viable route between them. The route may well be memorized by the colour and the direction

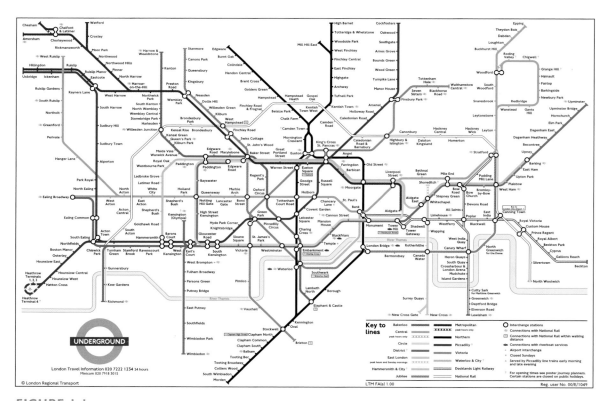

FIGURE 1.1

Contemporary map of the London Underground transportation system ('The Tube')

Source: *Reproduced by kind permission of London Transport Museum. Registered Exempt User No. 00/E/1049*

of the line(s) involved and any interchange station, or it may be memorized verbally as 'east on the blue line then west on the red line'. In this way a relevant portion of the underground system has been visualized and the resulting internal model – whatever its form – can be accessed during the journey to ensure arrival at the correct destination.

Sometimes we refer to the internal model as a **cognitive map** to distinguish it from the map of Figure 1.1 which is real in the sense of being an object pasted to the wall of the underground station. As Tversky (1993) points out;[2]

> *As mental constructs available to mental inspection, cognitive maps are presumed to be like real maps available to real inspection.*

With the underground map the task facilitated by visualization is that of planning a journey. In a simple – but true – sense the printed underground map is a visualization tool.

The second example, also supportive of visualization, is somewhat different in its aim. Its purpose is to elicit, from the viewer, a response of the form 'Ah HA' (the 'HA' being emphasized, prolonged and probably of higher pitch!), indicating that sudden insight has been obtained into some effect, insight that might well lead to significantly enhanced understanding or a new idea. The concept is illustrated in Figure 1.2, the origin of which is almost 200 years old but redrawn here for clarity. William Playfair, its author, wished to stress that, of the four great empires of his day, the British Empire was far too heavily taxed (Biderman, 1990). The left-hand uprights are proportional to gross national product and the right-hand uprights to tax income, so it is the *slope* of the connecting lines that draws attention to the point that Playfair was trying to make.

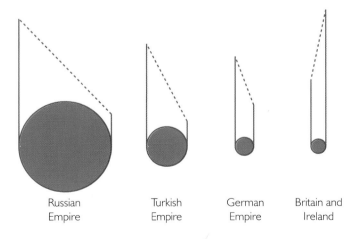

| Russian Empire | Turkish Empire | German Empire | Britain and Ireland |

FIGURE 1.2
William Playfair's circles, showing gross national product (left upright) and tax gathered (right upright)

---

[2] Tversky goes on to point out that the concept of a cognitive map may be too restrictive, and proceeds to discuss the interesting concept, to which we refer later, of Cognitive Collages.

1.3 Scientific visualization

There is a related, and somewhat overlapping field called 'scientific visualization' in which what is seen primarily relates to, and represents visually (usually in simulated 3D) a physical 'thing' such as a mountain range over which clouds are flowing or a girder in which the stress is of interest. Notwithstanding the fact that many of the techniques we discuss can usefully be applied in these situations, the need to display the physical 'thing' is not so important – and is often entirely irrelevant – in information visualization. In this book we are more concerned with abstract concepts such as price, stress, baseball scores, currency fluctuations and 'nearness to optimum' which, while undoubtedly associated with real physical things, are far more important than the view of those things. A currency trader knows perfectly well what a dollar bill looks like, but does not need to see its image (unless used for encoding purposes – see Chapter 4) while trading. Similarly, a study of baseball statistics (see Chapter 2) does not require an image of a baseball, whereas flow in a pipe is usually best displayed in the immediate context of the pipe itself. This book does not address the subject of scientific visualization, though many of the techniques discussed are relevant to it.

1.4 Data and information

Broadly speaking, we are concerned in this book with situations in which a body of data is available and a human being wishes to gain insight into that data: in other words, they wish to be *informed* by that data. It is important to make a clear distinction between data and information. The 'information explosion' so widely discussed is actually a data explosion: it is the derivation of information (or understanding, or insight) from the data that is difficult, and which we attempt to facilitate by means of visualization tools.

1.4.1 Data types

The data we wish to visualize can be as disparate as the details of houses in the files of an estate agent, a huge collection of data amassed by a supermarket, the network of stations on the Paris Metro and the multitude of complex relationships between the currents and voltages within a hifi. Usually, though not always, insight and knowledge are required because there is a task to be performed: buying a house, planning what brand of grapes to advertise as a special offer, getting to the Opera station, or designing a high-quality hifi.

The data will not always be *numerical*, though much of it is. It can be *ordinal*, as with things that are naturally ordered (such as the days of the week), or *categorical*, such as the names of animals where there is no order (for example, horse, zebra, antelope) (Figure 1.3).

FIGURE 1.3
Numerical,
ordinal and
categorical data

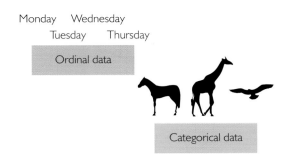

1.5 Examples

We begin by examining six examples of visualization, four from the nineteenth century, one from the early twentieth century and one of recent origin. In each case we briefly reflect upon the issues raised and, in apparent contradiction to an earlier exhortation, begin to use, without formal definition, some of the terminology that will become commonplace later in the book.

1.5.1 Taxation

The first example has already been introduced (Figure 1.2) and was created as long ago as 1801 by William Playfair. Here we have four objects, each with two *attributes* (gross national product and tax income), and the presentation is chosen to make one statement. It is the slope associated with the British Empire that stands out as the 'odd one out' and thereby makes the point for Playfair.

Many questions emerge. Is slope the best way of drawing attention to something that is different? How could Sir Edward have handled more attributes such as population and the sources of income. Would colour offer a good encoding mechanism?

1.5.2 Napoleon

Monsieur Minard, Napoleon's mapmaker, produced an illustration (Figure 1.4) of the famous march to, and retreat from, Moscow by Napoleon's army. The thickness of the brown line is proportional to the number of soldiers at any one location during the advance, and black similarly encodes the retreat. The toll on life is immediately obvious: of the 422,000 soldiers who started out, only 10,000 returned. The loss of life which occurred during the crossing of the Berezina river during the retreat (when many soldiers fell through the ice) is particularly striking. A contributory factor overall was the weather conditions which can be imagined from the temperature plot at the bottom of the illustration. Hardly, you may reflect, a good recruitment poster!

FIGURE 1.4
Minard's map of
Napoleon's
march to, and
retreat from,
Moscow

Source: *Tufte (1983)*

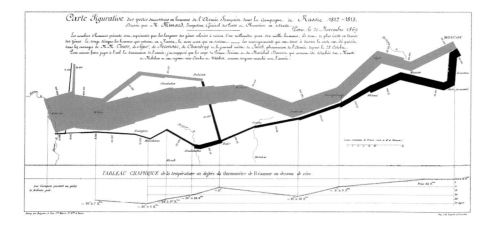

Minard's design triggers further questions. Why use the colours we see in Figure 1.4? Were they the only colours available? How does one strike a balance between simplicity and complexity – could additional interesting information have been included? Are there any locations where more detail might have been beneficial? If so, how could it have been included? Could temperature have been encoded differently? Anticipating later chapters, how could the illustration usefully be made interactive? Could Tchaikovsky's 1812 overture be effectively combined with the map?

1.5.3 Nightingale's roses

Florence Nightingale was the heroic nurse who went out to the front-line British Army hospitals in the Crimea in the mid-1850s, to tend the wounded and the sick (the latter were by far the majority). What is not widely known is that, as a result of her observations of the appalling conditions in those hospitals (and too graphic to repeat here), she persuaded a Sanitary Commission to undertake improvements and, furthermore, wrote a report (Nightingale, 1858)[3] to the British Government describing the unsatisfactory conditions and how they were improved.

The improvements she achieved are strikingly displayed in a rose-shaped diagram (Figure 1.5), which not only shows the number of deaths, month by month, in the British Army hospitals in the Crimea but also, to provide a basis of comparison (the dotted line), the number of deaths in Army hospitals in Manchester, England, during the same months. Each segment, whose subtended angle corresponds to elapsed time, has an area proportional to the number of deaths during that period. The effect of the new regime, begun in March 1855 ('Commencement of Sanitary Improvements' in Figure 1.5) is clearly displayed.

---

[3] Nightingale's book contains a fascinating appendix containing recipes. However, it is strongly recommended that details of the Crimean hospitals are not perused before eating the results of Nightingale's – or anyone else's – recipes.

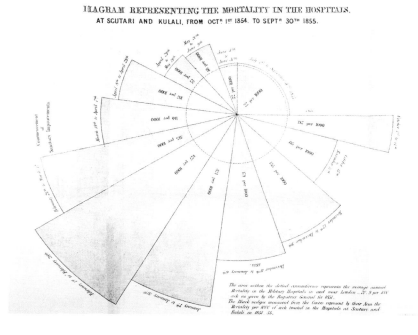

DIAGRAM REPRESENTING THE MORTALITY IN THE HOSPITALS.
AT SCUTARI AND KULALI, FROM OCT.ᵗ 1ˢᵗ 1854. TO SEPT.ᵗ 30ᵗʰ 1855.

FIGURE 1.5
Florence
Nightingale's
diagram
showing the
dramatic
reduction in the
death rates

Source: *Nightingale
(1858)*

1.5.4 An outbreak of cholera

There was an outbreak of cholera in London's Soho district in the year 1845.
The medical officer for London at that time, Dr John Snow, had the task of
bringing that outbreak under control. Although the detailed story behind John
Snow's investigation makes fascinating reading (Tufte, 1997), the relevance to
information visualization is clear from Figure 1.6. Here we see John Snow's map
of the area: black dots represent individual deaths from cholera and × marks the
positions of the water pumps. Snow observed that most of the deaths were concentrated around the Broad Street pump. His disablement of that pump was
followed by a decrease in the number of deaths from cholera. Workers at the
nearby brewery were noted to be relatively free from cholera, for reasons that
can be left to the reader's imagination.

It is interesting to speculate what other representations would have assisted
John Snow and how, with the availability of interactive computer graphics, a
present-day John Snow[4] could be assisted in his detective work.

1.5.5 Harry Beck's map

More recently (Figure 1.1) we have the invention, in 1931, of the famous
London Underground map by Harry Beck (Figure 1.7), an out-of-work draughts-
man 'who realized that when you are underground it doesn't matter where you
are. Beck saw – and what an intuitive stroke this was – that as long as the stations were presented in their correct sequence with their interchanges clearly

---

[4] A present-day John Snow would find, in Broad Street, neither pump nor (at the time of writing) a
cholera epidemic, merely a rather pleasant pub. Its name? The *John Snow*.

FIGURE 1.6
An 1845 map
of London's
Soho district,
showing deaths
from cholera
and the
locations of
water pumps

Source: *Tufte (1983)*

FIGURE 1.7
Harry Beck,
creator of the
familiar London
Underground
map

Source: *Ken Garland*

delineated, he could freely distort the scale and, indeed, abandon it altogether! He gave his map the orderly precision of an electrical wiring system, and in so doing created an entirely new, imaginary London that has very little to do with the disorderly geography of the city above' (Bryson, 1998). The story of Harry Beck and his map is a fascinating one (Garland, 1994).

Since 1931 the map has, not surprisingly, undergone many additions and modifications, but still retains Beck's brilliant idea; it is copied worldwide. Interestingly, we shall encounter the technique of distortion again in Chapter 7.

1.5.6 Tragically firefighting

A fire that is out of control is terrifying, and forest fires are especially awesome. On the night of 5 August 1949 (Maclean, 1992; Wainer, 1997), lightning struck trees in the Helena National Forest in the state of Montana (Figure 1.8). Sixteen Forest Service 'smoke jumpers' parachuted in to fight the blaze. But when they were close to the fire it became clear that the blaze was out of control and that their very survival depended upon quick action. But the fire moved faster, and eventually all the firefighters – within 200 yards of a safe haven at the top of Mann Gulch – were killed. The movement of the fire and the firefighters is tragically told by the two curves of Figure 1.9. One can imagine the race between firefighters and fire, especially after 5.52 pm, as the separation between the two curves becomes inexorably smaller, only 200 yards from safety. If only we could separate those two curves by 5 minutes or 200 yards . . . .

1.6 Computation

Although no computers were involved in any of the above examples (Spence, 1996), the simplicity of the illustrations nevertheless allows us to identify significant issues associated with information visualization, issues which are all the more pertinent when the power of the computer is available. The issues are many, and in most cases identify a chapter in which they are addressed in some detail.

1.6.1 Selection

From all the data available, each author selected that which was thought to be relevant to an envisaged task. A single message from Playfair, an historical record from Minard, a diagnostic tool from John Snow, and so on. What do we need to know about selection? Can it take place automatically? Is it useful sometimes to suppress information? Is selection very fundamental to information visualization? Some answers are provided in Chapter 2.

1.6.2 Representation

The author of a visualization tool must represent abstract things in some way. Playfair used contrasting slopes, Minard used colors, Nightingale invented 'roses' and Beck used colour and connectivity. Many other methods of encoding are

FIGURE 1.8
Map of part of
the Helena
National Forest
in Montana,
USA

Source: *Reprinted
from MacLean
(1992), which in turn
reprinted it from a
1952 U.S.
Department of
Agriculture report*

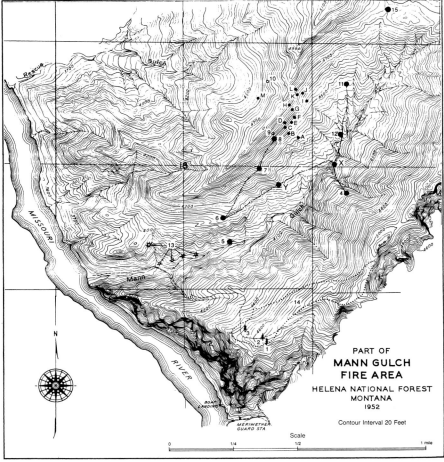

PART OF
**MANN GULCH
FIRE AREA**

HELENA NATIONAL FOREST
MONTANA
1952

Contour Interval 20 Feet

Scale

0   1/4   1/2   1 mile

LEGEND		BODIES FOUND	
1,2,3	Lightning struck trees.	A	Stanley J. Reba
4	Dodge met Harrison.	B	Silas R. Thompson
X	Dodge ordered crew to north side of Gulch.	C	Joseph B. Sylvia
Y	Dodge and Harrison rejoined crews; beginning of crew's race.	D	James O. Harrison
5	Jansson turned back.	E	Robert J. Bennett
6	Dodge and crew turned back.	F	Newton T. Thompson
7	Dodge ordered heavy tools dropped.	G	Leonard L. Piper
8	Dodge set escape fire.	H	Eldon E. Diettert
9	Dodge survived here.	I	Marvin L. Sherman
10	Rumsey and Sallee survived here.	J	David R. Navon
11	Jumping area (chutes assembled, burned).	K	Phillip R. McVey
12	Cargo assembly spot (burned).	L	Henry J. Thol, Jr.
13	Spot fires.	M	William J. Hellman
14	Approximate fire perimeter at time of jumping and cargo dropping (3:10–4:10 P.M.).		
15	Helecopter landing spot.		

possible, but which are useful? Can they be combined? What happens if an object has twenty attributes rather than two? Some answers are provided in Chapters 3 and 4, and by many examples throughout the text.

1.6.3 Presentation

Each author had to 'lay out' their data in some way. Harry Beck distorted the geography of the underground transportation network to make effective use of

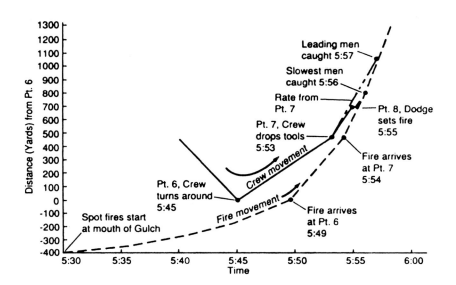

FIGURE 1.9
Movement of
fire and
firefighters
towards Mann
Gulch

Source: *MacLean*
(1992)

space and make the result more memorable, and Playfair lined up his empires so that the differences in slope were obvious. Often, we find we have more data than can easily be displayed at once in the limited area of the screen, especially with the emergence of Personal Digital Assistants and other hand-held devices such as mobile telephones. What can we do about this presentation problem? Some answers are provided in Chapter 7.

1.6.4 Scale and dimensionality

The illustrative examples examined so far involved very little data, whereas in many realistic situations in commerce and industry the volume of data into which insight is desirable can be huge. We must therefore be aware of ways in which scale influences the way in which visualization tools are designed. Chapters 5 and 7, in particular, address this issue. We must also consider the dimensionality of displayed data: how many features can be incorporated? Playfair considered two (national product and tax), and Minard more (location, temperature, size of army, direction, etc.): what techniques are available for handling high dimensionality?

1.6.5 Rearrangement, interaction and exploration

For someone viewing the examples presented in this chapter, the opportunity to explore the underlying data is either non-existent or rather limited, partly due to the relatively small amount of data involved and partly because there is no means of rearranging the data to provide a new and possibly much more valuable view of it. The ability to explore data by rearranging it interactively is so valuable that a great deal of effort has been invested in the invention and implementation of interactive visualization tools that harness this potential, as Chapters 2 and 5 in particular will emphasize.

1.6.6 Externalization

When introducing the concept of visualization we referred to the creation of an internal model or 'image' in the mind of the user. What the user actually sees, nowadays usually on a computer display, is called the externalization of the data. Clearly, the way in which data is externalized – usually by visual presentation (Tufte, 1983) – is crucial to the success with which visualization is achieved, a fact particularly emphasized in Chapter 4 but continuously underlined throughout the book.

1.6.7 Mental models

It has been pointed out that visualization is an essentially human activity, albeit supported most effectively by the computer, and we have referred to the internal model which the act of visualization creates within the mind of the viewer. If we can understand how this happens we are well placed to design visualization tools. Unfortunately our understanding is very limited, but in Chapter 6 we present a framework, broadly based upon models in human memory, that offers a useful tool for organized thought about information visualization.

1.6.8 Invention, experience and skill

All the visualization tools discussed in this book had to be invented or designed: they were not generated automatically. Nothing much has changed in this respect, and this is not surprising in view of the complexity and unpredictability of typical tasks, the fast changing 'palette' of interaction techniques available to the designer, and our lack of understanding of human–computer interaction in general. As Donald Norman remarked not too long ago, 'our lack of knowledge about Human Computer Interaction is appalling'. Nevertheless, inventions are usually followed by attempts to provide theoretical underpinnings which lead to a deeper understanding and pointers to possible future developments, and some of these underpinnings are presented in this book. But in the great majority of situations the design of a new visualization tool is a craft activity, the success of which depends upon the designer's understanding of the task for which the tool is intended, as well as the designer's possession of many and varied skills ranging from visual design to algorithm design.

1.7 A model

In the pre-computer age (Figure 1.10) the author of an image had to perform selection, representation and presentation according to his or her understanding of the task to be performed or the message to be conveyed: author and viewer were two different people. Now, with the availability of powerful computers (Figure 1.11), interactive control by a user – who is thereby to *some* extent the author of externalizations – can influence all these activities within a freedom defined by the architect of the visualization tool. It is the architect who has to design this interaction to constructively handle the range of interests that a user

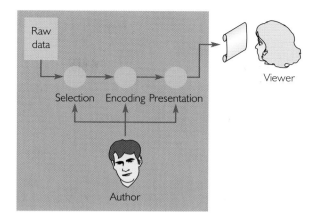

FIGURE 1.10
Pre-computer creation of a visualization tool

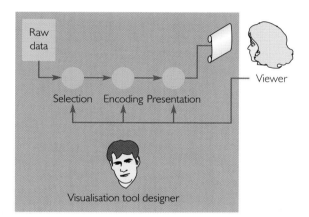

FIGURE 1.11
The creation and use of a computer-based visualization tool

may have. It is, in fact, that architect to whom this book is especially addressed, and whose motivation is reflected in the words of Proust:

The real voyage of discovery consists not in seeking new landscapes but in having new eyes.

CHAPTER 2

Rearrangement and Interaction

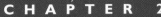

2.1 'A graphic . . . is a moment in the process of decision making'

Anyone who has seen, and especially *used*, a highly responsive interactive visualization tool will be struck by two features. First, that a mere *rearrangement* of how the data is displayed can lead to a surprising degree of additional insight into that data. Second, that the very property of interactivity can considerably enhance that tool's effectiveness, especially if the computer's response follows a user's action virtually immediately, say within a fraction of a second.

To illustrate the concept of rearrangement we begin with a simple example in which ten crops (for example, wheat, rice, beans . . .) have been subjected to seven treatments (for example, insecticide, . . .), and the improvement or otherwise noted. If improvement is coded black and degradation white, the result of the experiments might appear as in Figure 2.1(a), where crops are numbered from 1 to 10 and treatments designated by A to G. Note that we are here concerned with categorical data: the ordering has been imposed merely for convenience of reference.

It is probably fair to say that the likelihood of anyone gaining immediate insight from Figure 2.1(a) is negligible. Now, however, imagine the diagram to be cut into rows as shown in Figure 2.1(b) and for these rows to be rearranged in an order which assigns priority to placing black squares as high as possible, first in column A, then in column B, and so on (Figure 2.1(c)). In other words, rows with a black entry in column A are ordered first, followed by rows with such an entry in column B, and so on. In Figure 2.1(c) we see some sort of pattern beginning to emerge.

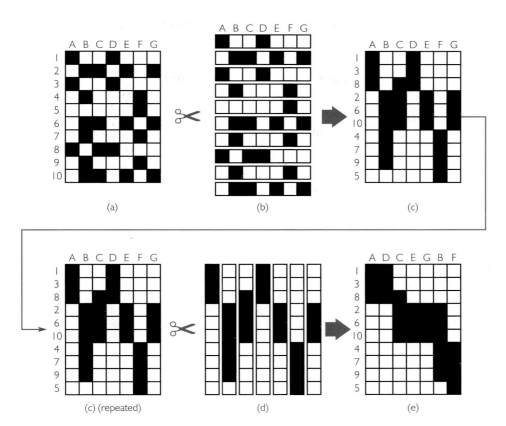

FIGURE 2.1
Rearrangement of data concerning the treatment of crops

If the same process is now repeated, starting with Figure 2.1(c) but with cuts (Figure 2.1(d)) to allow *columns* to be similarly rearranged, the result has the appearance of Figure 2.1(e). The same data is involved, but its presentation has changed: one can clearly perceive a pattern, showing that certain groups of treatments are appropriate to certain groupings of crops.[1]

It is at this point that the question 'OK, but what now?' may be asked. The most useful – as well as the most perceptive – answer was provided by Bertin (1981) who commented that:

> *A graphic is no longer 'drawn' once and for all: it is 'constructed' and reconstructed (manipulated) until all the relationships which lie within it have been perceived . . . a graphic is never an end in itself: it is a moment in the process of decision making.*

We have just seen, in Figure 2.1, one such 'reconstruction'. That there will typically be more is confirmed by Cleveland's (1985) comment that:

> *Graphing data needs to be iterative because we often do not know what to expect of the data; a graph can help discover unknown aspects of the data, and once the unknown is known, we frequently find ourselves formulating new questions about the data.*

---

[1] I'm most grateful to Bob Waddington for permission to use the material shown in Figure 2.1.

Thus, following inspection of Figure 2.1(e), a user – and especially a user in possession of domain knowledge (for example, a crop geneticist) – may decide upon further rearrangement or the addition of possibly relevant data. Here is the essence – and certainly quite often the excitement – of interactive visualization: a lively, iterative examination and interpretation of graphically presented data, in which rearrangement is an important part and the outcome is usually not predictable.[2]

2.2 The Table Lens

Our second example is drawn from baseball data, in particular that data contained in the *Baseball Encyclopedia Update 1997*. The data concerns 323 players, each associated with a row in a table; the columns of that table refer to attributes such as salary, position (in the baseball field) and hits. The Table Lens (Rao and Card, 1994) allows each column to be viewed as a histogram (Figure 2.2), and there is a facility whereby a name can be associated with a particular row of the histograms.

Clearly there are many ways in which the rows can be ordered. Alphabetic ordering, for example, would enable a particular player to be located with ease. A more interesting reordering however, is shown in Figure 2.2. Here, the rows have first been reordered according to the (ordinal) attribute 'position' and then according to 'number of hits'. It therefore shows the number of hits achieved by each batting position. By examining the 'position' and 'hits'

FIGURE 2.2
A Table Lens displaying baseball data

Source: *Inxight Software, Inc.*

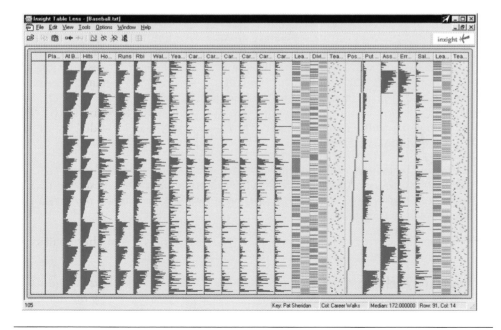

---

[2] Rearrangement, of course, is not always beneficial, as when a well-intentioned cleaner 'tidies up' one's desk (Malone, 1983)!

columns one can see that different batsmen in the same position are character-ized by a range of batting skills. The Table Lens possesses the advantage, as far as ease of use is concerned, that it is based on a table, a concept with which most people are familiar.

We shall revisit the Table Lens again in Chapter 7 to identify additional ben-eficial features: in the context of rearrangement, however, an important question to be answered now is *how* the rows are reordered. The reordering action chosen by Rao and Card (1994) is simple, and illustrated in Figure 2.3(a): a movement of the mouse down the column which is to be ordered. The move-ment need not be precisely vertical. Another example of how a gesture with the mouse can lead to rearrangement is shown in Figure 2.3(b): a 'tick' with the mouse in the column associated with attribute *B* followed by a similar tick for attribute A triggers the generation of a new column containing a histogram of the values of *B/A*.

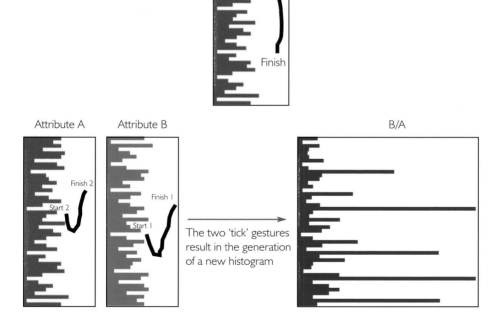

FIGURE 2.3
(a) Reordering of the entries in the Table Lens (b) Calculation of a new column in the Table Lens

2.3 Affordances

The example of the Table Lens illustrates an important aspect of rearrangement to which the designer of an information visualization tool must give attention: it is called **affordance**. The concept is perhaps most effectively introduced by a physical example taken from Norman (1988). You are approaching a door through which you eventually want to pass. The door, and the manner in which it is secured to the wall, permits opening by pushing it from its 'closed' position. We say that the door *affords* (or *allows*, or *is for*) opening by pushing. On approaching that door (Figure 2.4) you observe a flat plate fixed to it at waist height on the 'non-hinge' side, and possibly some sticky fingermarks on its otherwise polished surface. You deduce – correctly in this case – that the door is meant to be pushed open: you therefore push on the plate, whereupon the door opens and you pass through. Here, there is a *perceived* affordance, triggered by the sight of the plate and the fingermarks, that is identical with the *actual* affordance. Note that the affordance we discuss is neither the door nor the plate: it is a *property* of the door ('the door affords opening by pushing').

FIGURE 2.4
The door is perceived, correctly, to afford opening by pushing

You now have to proceed through a second door, and observe (Figure 2.5) that it has a handle, again at about waist height. Your interpretation is that you are meant to pull the handle towards you, thereby opening the door. Though a reasonable interpretation, it happens to be incorrect – the door does not move. You try pushing it instead, again to no avail. After some exploration you then discover that the door opens by sliding (it *affords* opening by sliding), and that the correct action is to 'turn' the handle and apply a horizontal force. In this situation the *perceived* affordance (that the door affords opening by pulling) is not the same as the *actual* affordance (the door affords opening by sliding). Clearly, designers of doors, and particularly their mechanisms and associated devices such as handles, will try to ensure that perceived and actual affordances are identical.[3] It is important to note from these simple examples that experience and convention influence one's perception of affordance.

---

[3] Those who are required quite frequently to stay in hotels may well wonder whether designers of shower controls are familiar with the difference between perceived and actual affordances.

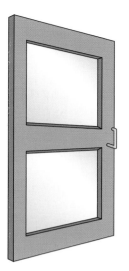

FIGURE 2.5
The door is perceived, incorrectly, to afford opening by pulling

In designing interactive displays to facilitate a beneficial rearrangement of the visual presentation of data, the same design objective is present: the designer should ensure, as far as possible, that perceived and actual affordances are identical. But that is not always easy to achieve. As an illustration we choose (Figure 2.6) the familiar scroll controls associated with a word-processing application. A 'mouse-down' on the control **A** (that is, anywhere within the rectangle containing the triangular arrow) will, for example, cause the contents of the display to scroll downwards until 'mouse-up' occurs. Thus, the *actual* affordance of scrolling must be deduced by the user. In this case the sensitive control icon **A** is chosen by the interaction designer with the expectation that the perceived affordance of scrolling will be identical to the actual affordance of scrolling. Nevertheless, the interaction designer will be aware that an understanding of the icon's function depends upon many factors including convention and how suggestive the icon is.

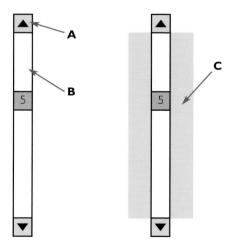

FIGURE 2.6
Scroll controls familiar from a word-processing application

In some cases a perceived affordance is difficult to formulate, sometimes because the relevant control may be far from obvious. An example is provided by area **B**, the rectangular area extending from the upper edge of the page indicator to the lower edge of the 'scroll-down' control. At a first glance it is not obvious if a mouse-click on this area will achieve anything at all. However, through exploration or training it is found that a mouse-click in **B** causes flipping to the extent of one page.[4] Moreover, prolonged mouse-down in **B** causes page flipping to continue at a convenient rate until terminated by a mouse-up.

Other controls may not even be completely externalized: to ease the user's task and avoid demanding precisely vertical movement of the cursor within the relatively thin scroll-bar, it is often the case that the mouse-down drag can deviate considerably from the scroll-bar (within area **C**) and yet be interpreted as being *on* the scroll-bar (Figure 2.6).

With the Table Lens (Figure 2.2) the actual affordance is far from obvious and must be learned. Nevertheless, once learned, considerable insight into the underlying table of data is possible, as is fluency of use.

2.4 Hair and eyes: the Mosaic Display

The two illustrative rearrangements presented above – the crop treatments and the Table Lens – were intentionally simple, even though the Table Lens offers other useful functions which are discussed in Chapter 7. We now examine another example of rearrangement called the Mosaic Display (Hartigan and Kleiner, 1981, 1984; Unwin *et al.*, 1996; Unwin, 1999).

Once upon a time, as all interesting stories seem to begin, a lecturer in statistics (Snee, 1974) recorded, for each of his 592 students, the colour of the student's eyes and hair. The result is shown in Table 2.1, from which little insight can immediately be gained. Instead, we consider (Figure 2.7) a diagram

TABLE 2.1 Data concerning the hair and eye colour of 592 students

Eye colour	Hair colour				Total
	Black	Brown	Red	Blond	
Brown	68	119	26	7	220
Blue	20	84	17	94	215
Hazel	15	54	14	10	93
Green	5	29	14	16	64
Total	108	286	71	127	592

---

[4] Except for the last line, to provide continuity.

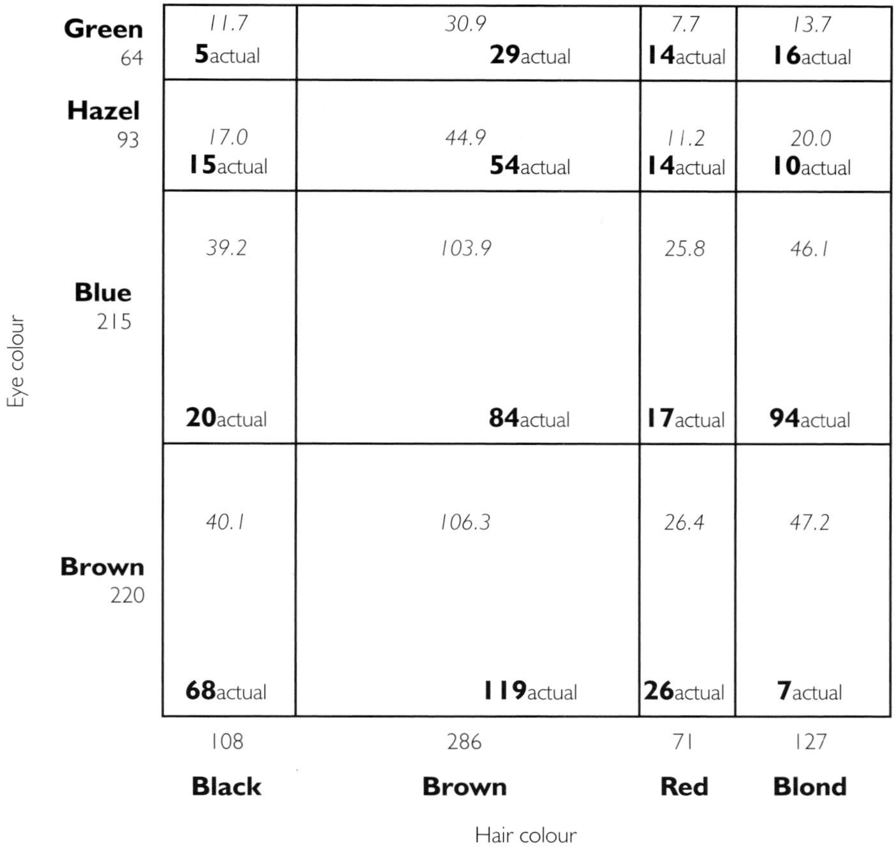

Eye colour	Black	Brown	Red	Blond
Green 64	11.7 / **5**actual	30.9 / **29**actual	7.7 / **14**actual	13.7 / **16**actual
Hazel 93	17.0 / **15**actual	44.9 / **54**actual	11.2 / **14**actual	20.0 / **10**actual
Blue 215	39.2 / **20**actual	103.9 / **84**actual	25.8 / **17**actual	46.1 / **94**actual
Brown 220	40.1 / **68**actual	106.3 / **119**actual	26.4 / **26**actual	47.2 / **7**actual
	108	286	71	127

Hair colour

FIGURE 2.7 Diagram showing all combinations of eye and hair colouring

to be constructed so that each rectangle, of which there are 16 corresponding to all combinations of eye and hair colour, has a height proportional to the number of students having a given eye colour, and a width proportional to the number of students having a given hair colour. Now suppose – incorrectly, as we shall see – that a person's eye color is independent of hair colour: the area of each of the 16 rectangles in Figure 2.7 (and indicated by the small *italic* inscribed values) would then be a measure of the probability of occurrence of all combinations of eye and hair colour. In fact, these values are those probabilities multiplied by the total number of students, so that the total is 592, the number of students.

The inscribed numbers, however, do not correspond to the data in Table 2.1, because it transpires that eye and hair colour are not independent. The actual numbers, taken from Table 2.1, are shown **bold** and labeled 'actual' in Figure 2.7, and are seen to be different and in many cases very different, from the 'independent' numbers. The areas of the 16 rectangles are therefore misleading. A simple modification of Figure 2.7 is all that is required to provide a far more informative presentation: in the absence of independence the so-called Mosaic Display of Figure 2.8, which is similar to a divided bar chart, can provide more insight (Hartigan and Kleiner, 1981, 1984; Friendly, 1994). Here, the width of

FIGURE 2.8
A Mosaic Display, with areas proportional to the actual numbers possessing various combinations of eye and hair colour

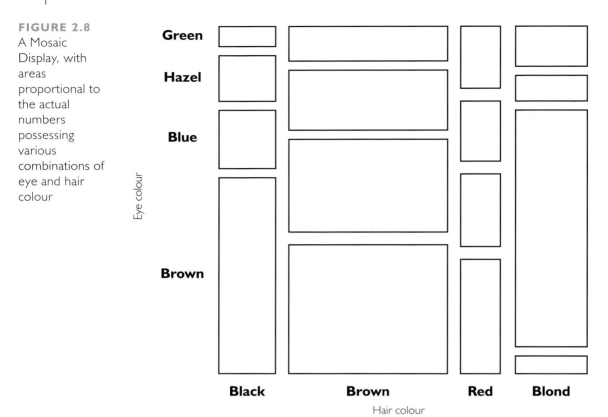

each 'tile' is still proportional to the relative occurrence of the four hair colours, but now the height is governed by the *actual* number of students with the appropriate eye colour. Unlike Figure 2.7, where equal heights indicate an assumed independence, the mosaic display of Figure 2.8 reflects the actual dependence and provides more insight. Certain tiles stand out: there are, for example, more blue-eyed blonds and brown-eyed black-haired people than would occur under independence. With the exception of the first and last rows, the rows are not aligned, which makes it harder to make comparisons within eye-colour groups. This drawback can be remedied by generating a new mosaic plot with the eye colours determining the widths and hair colours determining the heights.

Further rearrangement can be helpful. Figure 2.9 recognizes the deviation from independence between eye and hair colour. Shades of red and green indicate the extent of the deviation from independence, and the ordering of the eye and hair colours (which, of course, are categorical and not ordinal variables) has been chosen to ensure that deviations from independence have an 'opposite-corner' pattern. Extensions of the mosaic display are treated in Chapter 3: the underlying concept is first introduced here to provide yet another example of the value of rearrangement.

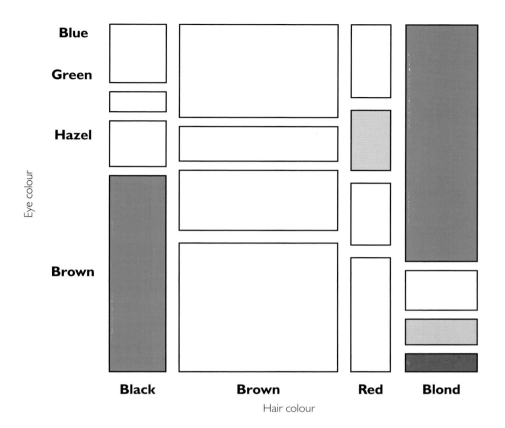

FIGURE 2.9
In the Mosaic
Display, colour
indicates the
deviation from
independence

2.5 Network data

A dramatic benefit arising from the rearrangement of data can also be associated with 'network' or 'connectivity' data. Suppose that the telephone calls made and received by 13 people (labeled 'A' to 'M') during a specific period are recorded and presented in a table (Table 2.2). Even a careful study of Table 2.2 will typically fail to disclose any interesting pattern or features of interest. Even when represented in the form of a node-link graph (Figure 2.10) it is still not easy to discern a pattern in the same data.

However, if the data is processed in a very simple way to identify unconnected subgraphs, and represented by a node-link diagram (Figure 2.11), we begin to see interesting features. While their interpretation cannot at this stage be deduced it is clear that there are three distinct groups of telephone users between which no telephonic communication took place during the time period of the recording. If the duration and/or frequency of each call was additionally recorded, then the encoding of this information, for example by line width, could provide additional insight (Figure 2.12(a)); so also could colour-coding to represent the proportion of outgoing and incoming calls (Figure 2.12(b)).

TABLE 2.2 Telephone communication between 13 people

Originator	Receiver
A	H
C	L
I	M
B	E
F	H
G	I
I	B
B	M
K	B
G	B
K	E
C	J
D	C
F	A
J	L

FIGURE 2.10 A node-link graph representing telephone communication between people

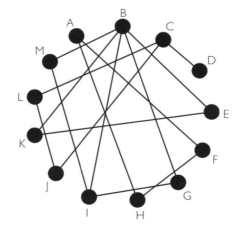

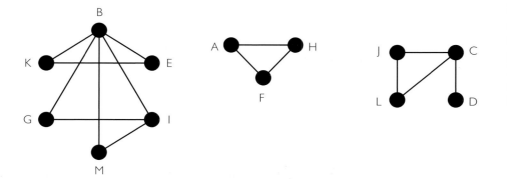

FIGURE 2.11
A rearrange-
ment of the
graph of Figure
2.10, identifying
an interesting
feature

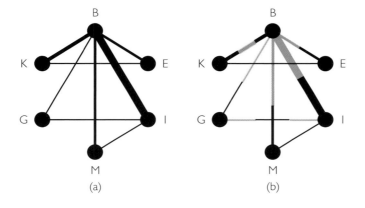

(a) (b)

FIGURE 2.12
Methods of
encoding
parameters
characterizing
a link

2.6 Selective manipulation

The display of Figure 2.13 shows the geographic location of a supply distribution
network for a relief effort in a large-scale crisis, as presented by the Selective
Display and Manipulation (SDM) system (Chuah *et al.*, 1995). Supply centres
are represented by cylinders, main routes between them by dark lines on the
'floor plane' and shelters where supplies are needed by rectangular bars. Heights
indicate material quantities. Figure 2.13 might be regarded as a very 'busy' and
cluttered display, attracting the comment that perhaps too much data is being
presented concurrently, with the attendant danger of occlusion. On the other
hand, it could be argued that one's interpretation of (say) the green items
depends at times on the layout of the purple items, and that the display of only
one type of item would lead to an impoverished display. A useful technique
under these circumstances (Figure 2.14) is that of 'raising' the reference level
for one class of item so that it can be examined in a clutter-free manner, though
still within context. Shrinking the width of irrelevant bars is also possible, and
can be helpful. A typical drawback of a three-dimensional presentation – the difficulty of comparing patterns, widths and heights that are at different 'distances'
from the user – is overcome by allowing selected bars associated with a user-
drawn reference line to be projected onto a two-dimensional presentation that
allows comparisons to be made (Figure 2.15).

FIGURE 2.13
Display of the geographic location of a supply distribution network for a relief effort in a large-scale crisis

Source: *Chuah (1995), Chuah et al. © 1995 Association for Computing Machinery, Inc. Reprinted by permission*

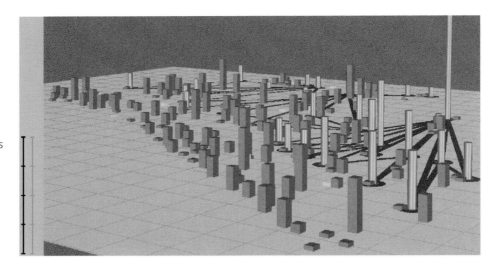

FIGURE 2.14
Raising a reference for one class of item allows that class to be examined more easily

Source: *Chuah (1995), Chuah et al. © 1995 Association for Computing Machinery, Inc. Reprinted by permission*

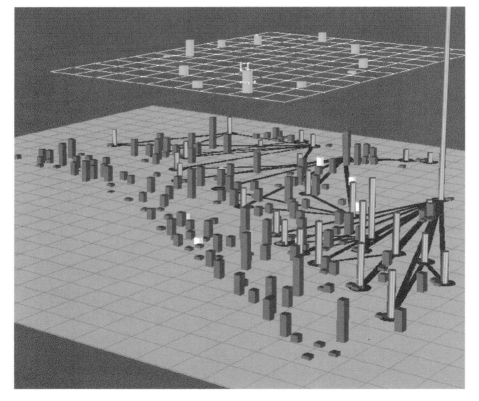

FIGURE 2.15
A reference
line enables
comparisons
to be made

Source: *Chuah
(1995), Chuah et al.
© 1995 Association
for Computing
Machinery, Inc.
Reprinted by
permission.*

2.7 Algorithms

Many visualization techniques are only made possible by algorithms of considerable complexity which operate upon available data. We choose for illustration an
example that relates to a user's search among a collection of documents to identify one (or a group) which is particularly appropriate to that user's interest.[5]
Obviously the user does not want to have to read through a large number of documents – and especially those which are of little or no interest – to find the most
interesting one; rather, they might be happy instead to supply either some keywords or an existing document known to characterize their interest to some
degree and then, via an effective visualization tool, either discover a suitable
document or be guided towards a revision of their query. Thus, as with other
examples in this chapter, the same data is available but is selected, and its presentation rearranged, to suit the task being undertaken.

An underlying problem with searches for interesting documents is the huge
amount of data required to characterize the word content of a single document.
Words within a document will typically be examined to determine the frequency

---

[5] A more detailed discussion of this task is the subject of Chapter 10.

of their occurrence, often resulting in a collection (a 'vector') of thousands of numbers, each denoting the frequency of occurrence of a particular word. Comparison of that vector with keywords supplied by a user will enable the relevance of that document to be estimated. Fortunately, not only are algorithms available for carrying out such characterizations and comparisons, but others – also of considerable complexity – are available which can represent the documents in two-dimensional space on a conventional display. Frequently, this representation is so arranged that 'similar' documents are represented by points which are close together, whereas those with little in common are positioned far apart, and for these points to be displayed (Chalmers, 1993) in a 'landscape' presentation (Figure 2.16) which permits interactive interrogation. Chalmers *et al.* (1996) have proposed two features of a landscape presentation to aid search (Figure 2.17). One is to colour the area bounding those documents which are of interest, and the other, shown at the top of the display in the form of miniatures, is to display previous results and associated keywords; a visible trace of recent landscapes can be valuable in suggesting new or modified queries. In many visualization tools a visible record of earlier steps has often been found to be useful when a step-by-step approach to some goal is involved.

FIGURE 2.16
A landscape presentation of data about documents
Source: *After Matthew Chalmers*

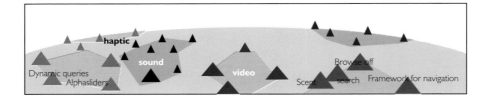

2.8 The nature of rearrangement

Rearrangement can occur in different ways. In the Table Lens and other examples a new presentation appeared following a **discrete** command of some sort. But there is another class of useful rearrangement in which the display of data is **dynamically** rearranged. Two modes are of interest. In one, a smooth **manually controlled** rearrangement enables cause and effect to be displayed simultaneously, often to good effect. In the other mode, rearrangement is **automated**, leaving the user free to concentrate upon interpretation. We briefly examine these two modes of dynamic rearrangement.

2.8.1 Dynamic manual rearrangement

Insight into the relation between two or more quantities is often sought by the manual variation of one variable and concurrent observation of the consequent variation of one or more remaining variables. An example is provided by the activity of engineering design.

The design of a physical object, whether it be a radio or a kettle, is not a straightforward process but, as Chapter 9 will demonstrate in detail, is one that can benefit considerably from information visualization. Figure 2.18 shows part

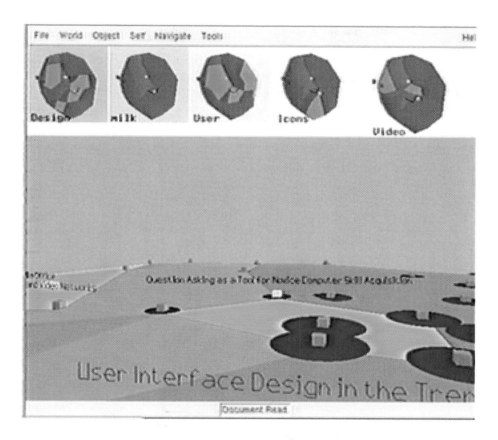

FIGURE 2.17
A visible trace
of earlier steps
in the
examination of
colour-coded
landscapes

Source: *Matthew
Chalmers*

FIGURE 2.18
The red area
of this display
contains all
acceptable
designs of an
artefact and
the yellow box
contains all the
manufactured
samples

of a display that can be of value to a designer. A point within the display area represents a design, since its projection onto the horizontal axis is one dimension of the object being designed (the base area of a kettle, for example), and its projection on the vertical axis is another – perhaps the thickness of the kettle. The red part of the display contains points (that is, designs) that satisfy the customer: one of the boundaries of the red region might correspond to the cost of manufacturing the kettle. But because a mass-produced object such as a kettle cannot be manufactured with infinite precision, the many points representing the many mass-produced kettles will lie *anywhere* within the yellow box. There is therefore much to be gained (especially 100 per cent manufacturing yield) if the yellow box can be made to lie completely within the red region.

The designer can easily move the box (in this case vertically) so that more designs lie within the red region. However, by exploration, the designer has discovered that the picture can be changed to that of Figure 2.19, to provide a larger red area, by choosing a new value for a third dimension of the object – perhaps the height of the kettle. The yellow box has not only been better placed with regard to the red region, but can now be positioned within a much larger red region, ensuring a high manufacturing yield.

As with the other examples in this chapter, no new data is being generated or acquired: here the designer is simply exercising a design freedom by selecting, for view, a different subset of the data, in this case such that more yield can be achieved.

FIGURE 2.19
Alteration of the design leads to a greater area (red) in which acceptable designs can lie enabling the yellow box to be positioned to lead to a greater manufacturing yield

2.8.2 *Dynamic automated rearrangement*

Figure 2.20 is a display which shows the designer of an electronic circuit the extent to which each component within it affects the circuit's overall performance. Following the designer's sketch of the circuit diagram on a computer display (Figure 2.20(a)), the area of the circle superimposed[6] on a component's symbol (Figure 2.20(b)) provides an indication of the change in circuit performance that would result from a 1 per cent change in component value. This effect is termed 'sensitivity' and the circles are known as 'sensitivity circles' (Spence and Drew, 1971; Spence and Apperley, 1977). Such an indication of sensitivity can be immensely valuable to the designer.

However, if the circuit is a hifi, the designer is interested in the sensitivity to each component *over a range of frequencies* reaching from bass to treble, so that a static display, as in Figure 2.20(b), is of limited value. A simple solution to

---

[6] In the actual presentation the shape of the symbol can be discerned through the circle, thereby removing any doubt in the designer's mind about the nature of the component to which a circle refers.

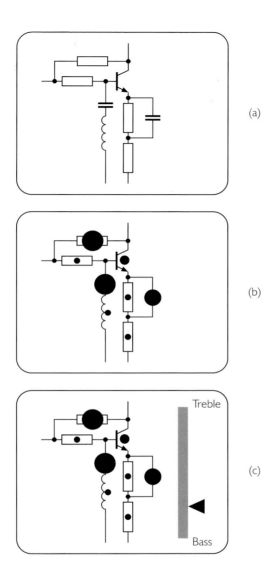

FIGURE 2.20
(a) Part of an electronic circuit diagram drawn on a computer display
(b) Circles provide a qualitative indication of the sensitivity of the circuit's performance to a change in each component
(c) A frequency indicator allows animation to display sensitivity as a function of frequency

the accommodation of an additional variable (frequency) is to employ anima-tion: to change the size of the circles as the frequency is automatically varied over a range of interest (Figure 2.20(c)). As the frequency indicator on the right moves smoothly up and down the frequency scale between bass and treble limits, the circle sizes vary accordingly. A designer's observation of which circles are large or small at which parts of the frequency range can immensely enhance their understanding of the circuit. The scanning rate – in other words, the speed of animation – requires careful choice: if circle sizes change too rapidly the designer may fail to comprehend the meaning of the changing circles: too slow and the designer has difficulty in integrating what is seen on the display into a useful mental model. An animation period of about eight seconds was found by experience to be optimum.

For a particular electronic circuit the visualization tool shown in Figure 2.20 displayed a sudden, substantial but temporary increase in the size of two circles. This unexpected result was noticed with some surprise by the designer, but quickly recognized as an indication of 'resonance'. This phenomenon is perhaps more familiar from the example of the destructive oscillation of the Tacoma Narrows bridge, and is equally undesirable in an electronic amplifier: a hifi emitting a constant whistle does not lead to customer satisfaction! Here is an example of an animated rearrangement of data leading to *discovery*. Fortunately for the designer, the frequency on the bass-to-treble scale could also be adjusted *manually*, and the precise frequency of resonance read directly from a numerical display beside the frequency scale.

2.9 Conclusion

We have seen, from many examples, how interactive rearrangement of the way in which data is presented can provide an opportunity for additional insight into that data. We have examined categorical data (crops and treatments, eye and hair colour), numerical data (baseball statistics), topological data (telephone connections), symbolic representations (sensitivity circles and complex geographical operations) and textual data (landscapes), merely as representative examples rather than to establish an exhaustive categorization. Many other examples exist, a particularly impressive one having to do with the 'O'-ring disaster in the fated Challenger shuttle (Tufte, 1997). In the chapters which follow, extensive use is made of this potential, and many other examples will be encountered.

CHAPTER 3

Interpretation of Quantitative Data

3.1 Content

As explained in the Preface, the primary *raison d'être* of this book is the presentation of those advances in information visualization that have been made possible, mainly during the decade from 1990 to 2000, by the emergence of inexpensive powerful computers, high-quality graphics, plentiful memory and responsive interaction. The interpretation of quantitative data by visual means has, of course, been proceeding over a much longer period, as evidenced by the classical works of Sir Ronald Fisher, John Tukey, Bertin and, most recently, Cleveland and McGill. This body of knowledge is certainly relevant to the reader. However, in view of its extent as well as the declared focus and readership of this book, that established knowledge will be selectively summarized here rather than discussed exhaustively. The aim of this chapter is to provide, for a wide readership, an introductory palette of useful techniques, but one which can be extended and underpinned by reference to existing texts according to the reader's interests.[1]

---

[1] Frequently referenced texts include those by Bertin (1981), Cleveland (1993, 1994), and Cleveland and McGill (1988). The reader is also referred to Card *et al.* (1999) for more recent comment.

3.2 Overview

An overview of this chapter can be obtained by considering the illustrative task of selecting one object from many on the basis of the numerical values of their attributes. An example is the purchase of a new car: here the attributes will include price, passenger capacity, petrol consumption and other quantitative measures.[2] The problem faced by the designer of an appropriate visualization tool is that of presenting the data, and allowing it to be rearranged, in such a way as to facilitate a decision.

3.3 Dimensionality

The difficulty of designing an interactive display is strongly influenced by the number of attributes – more generally referred to as variables – involved, and sometimes referred to as the dimensionality of the problem. If the cars are characterized by only one attribute (for example, cost) we are said to be dealing with univariate data and the design of the visualization tool is relatively – though not entirely – straightforward. If two attributes are involved we are said to be handling bivariate data, and the task of the visualization tool designer is a little more challenging. It is at this point that one is reminded of the African tribe whose language has words for 'one' and 'two', but only their word for 'many' for any number greater than two, because the task of enhancing a user's understanding of trivariate data (three attributes) suddenly becomes much more taxing. Indeed, in view of the many and varied situations in which more than three attributes are involved (hypervariate data) it is usually preferable, for trivariate data, to address the problem posed by *many* attributes where, as for that African tribe, 'many' is any number greater than two.

In what follows we shall, in fact, follow the taxonomy just introduced and consider, in turn, univariate, bivariate, trivariate and hypervariate data.[3]

3.4 Univariate data

Let us suppose there are 30 cars associated with some selection we have to make, and that they are characterized by the numerical value of just one attribute, that of price; here we have an example of a collection of measurements or attributes of a single quantitative variable. The details could be presented in a table (Table 3.1) or, almost certainly more effectively, in the form of points against some scale (Figure 3.1(a)). Space considerations will determine whether the corresponding objects can be labeled to enhance comprehension

---

[2] The fact that, in real life, the final choice may be heavily influenced by non-quantitative features such as colour and shape is not, as we shall see, a trivial consideration (see Chapter 5).

[3] This is, in fact, the taxonomy and pedagogical approach used by Cleveland (1993).

TABLE 3.1 The price and make of a collection of cars

Car	Price (£)
BMW	51,395
Mercedes	50,850
Mercedes	41,000
Saab	39,085
BMW	38,000
Rolls	36,950
BMW	34,550
Morgan	32,000
Rover	31,300
Ford	29,250
Saab	28,750
Mercedes	28,000
Ford	27,600
Ford	25,950
Land Rover	24,000
Jeep	23,200
Nissan	20,000
Vauxhall	18,500
Nissan	17,400
Ford	17,000
Ford	16,500
Nissan	15,500
Ford	14,950
Ford	12,000

(Figure 3.1(b)). Both examples in Figure 3.1 have useful features; the lowest and highest values are easily noted, the general distribution is clear and any 'bunching' is obvious.

Interpretation may be eased by introducing various forms of aggregation, for example by indicating the average of all the prices. Particularly valuable are Tukey Box Plots (Figure 3.2) in which the box indicates the 25th, 50th and 75th percentiles, the bars the 10th and 90th percentiles, and where any 'outliers' beyond the latter two percentiles are shown individually. An alternative is to retain all the individual points, and simply superimpose indications of the same percentiles (Figure 3.3). Other presentations of the same data, and involving aggregation, are possible (Tufte, 1983), and one is illustrated in Figure 3.4.

FIGURE 3.1
(a) Univariate
data plotted
against a scale
(b) Labeling of
the data points
may be difficult

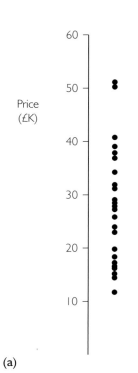

(a)

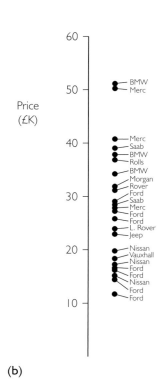

(b)

FIGURE 3.2
Tukey Box Plot
representation
of univariate
data

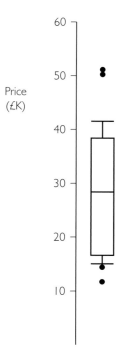

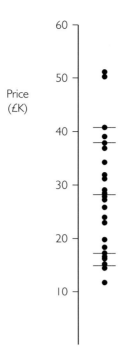

FIGURE 3.3
An alternative representation of key percentiles

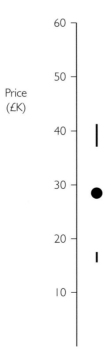

FIGURE 3.4
An alternative representation of the Tukey Box Plot

Yet another form of aggregation is the histogram (Figure 3.5) of which extensive use will be made later in the book. Tufte (1983) discusses various ways of enhancing a histogram's appearance. As we shall see later, a slider positioned below the histogram (Figure 3.6) can compactly contain aggregate data such as the position of an average and a variance (Eick, 1994).

FIGURE 3.5
Representation of univariate data by a histogram

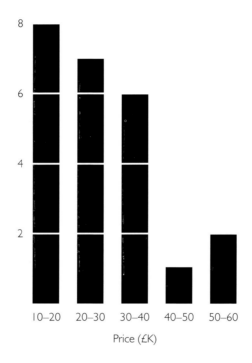

FIGURE 3.6
Incorporation of aggregate data – here the average and variance – within the scale

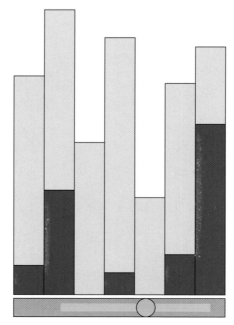

The number of data points can be – and usually is – quite large, in which case the ability to zoom to examine selected ranges in more detail can be valuable (Figure 3.7). Simple zooming, however, only allows a user to see bigger blobs: a much more effective operation is logical zooming, wherein more and more detail is revealed as magnification increases (Figure 3.8), an activity we shall later call semantic zooming.

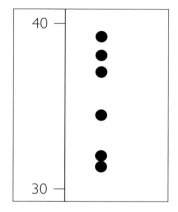
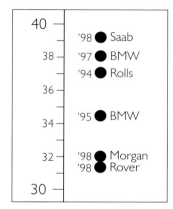

FIGURE 3.7
Result of zooming into univariate data

FIGURE 3.8
Result of a logical zoom

3.5 Bivariate data

A conventional approach to the visualization and interpretation of bivariate data is typified by a two-dimensional plot (Figure 3.9) of one variable against the other, a presentation called a scatterplot. In the house-hunting example shown a user can clearly identify global trends (*Price* generally increases with *Number of Bedrooms*) and local features such as trade-offs, as well as outliers that could prove both unexpected and worth further investigation (such as the five-bedroom house selling for £50,000).

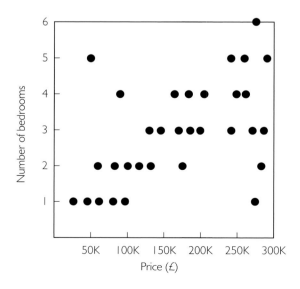

FIGURE 3.9
A scatterplot

In situations in which one of the two variables is controllable, and the data is thereby grouped, the box plot approach can again assist interpretation. In the example of Figure 3.10 one of the variables is the leading digit (of three) selected by a player in the New Jersey lottery, and the vertical axis is the payoff (Becker and Chambers, 1984). It is clear, for example, that the payoffs for three-digit numbers starting with a zero tend to be high, which means that those who bet avoid them. The plot also suggests that odd first digits are preferred to even ones.

FIGURE 3.10
Box plots used to represent bivariate data

Source: *Redrawn from Cleveland (1985)*

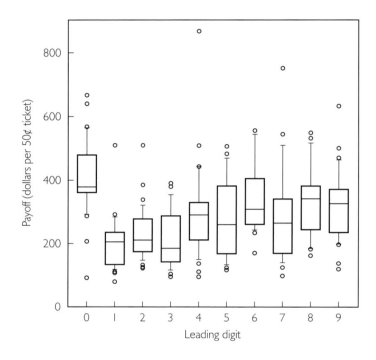

An approach to the display of bivariate data, and one which is extensively exploited later in the book (especially for hypervariate data) involves the use of histograms. While a separate histogram (Figure 3.11(a)) associated with each variable is of limited use as it stands, two enhancements can lead to an extremely useful visualization tool, and one whose value is enhanced by its application to hypervariate data. We first provide, below each histogram, a scale with adjustable limits by means of which a subset of the data can be identified (Figure 3.11(b)). Secondly, we ensure that the objects so identified by *both* sets of limits are colour-coded (Figure 3.11(b)). The display now becomes much more valuable since the influence of one variable on the other can be manually explored. An apparently minor modification in which selected (red) objects are 'ranged down' (Figure 3.11(c)) considerably enhances the value of the linked histograms, an advantage that can readily be appreciated when used dynamically. It is not difficult, as we shall see in Chapter 5, to arrange additionally for the manual adjustment of a *range* of variable *A* up and down the scale (that is, the limits move together), allowing a global impression of the relation

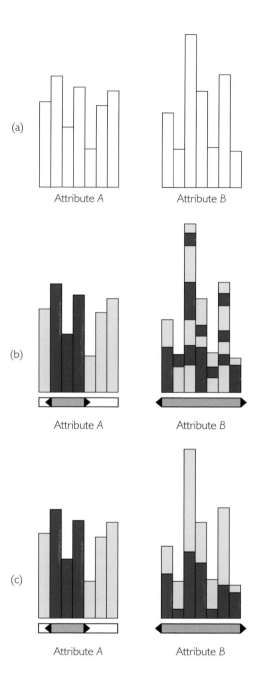

FIGURE 3.11
(a) Histograms
of two
attributes
(b) Histograms
with adjustable
limits for
selection
purposes
(c) Selected
objects are
'ranged down'
for easier
interpretation

between *A* and *B* to be gained. The enormous value of *dynamically* adjusted selection emphasizes the differences between visualization tools that are **passive** (for example, Minard's map), **active** (where a single action causes rearrangement) and **dynamic**, where continuous movement of a control causes continuous rearrangement.

3.6 Trivariate data

Living as we do in a three-dimensional world one would imagine that a three-dimensional display of data would be regarded as 'natural' in some sense and therefore ideal for the display of data. While that might be true to some extent in the (usually expensive) context of virtual reality, the problem arises with the fundamentally *two-dimensional* representation of a three-dimensional space. Figure 3.12, for example, provides a two-dimensional view of a three-dimensional space in which four houses have been placed according to their numerical values of three attributes, *Price*, number of *Bedrooms* and *Time* to reach one's

FIGURE 3.12
A 2D
presentation of
a 3D plot

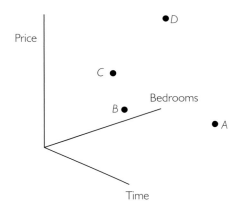

workplace. But can we decide if *A* has a greater value of *Price* than *B*? No, we can't. To answer this and similar questions we could project the points onto all pairs of axes (Figure 3.13). More usefully, however, we can rearrange these plots in an organized manner to form a scatterplot matrix (Figure 3.14).

FIGURE 3.13
Projection of
the points in
Figure 3.12
onto all pairs
of axes

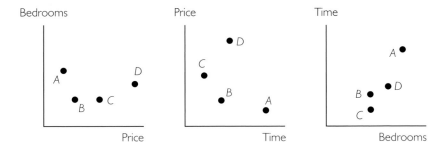

At first sight the value of a scatterplot matrix is not apparent. Since the matrix contains as many scatterplots as there are pairs of parameters it can become a little unwieldy for more than about five parameters. Moreover, we are faced with the drawback that for *N* objects with three attributes we now have a collection of 3*N* points; if there are 4 attributes the number of points increases

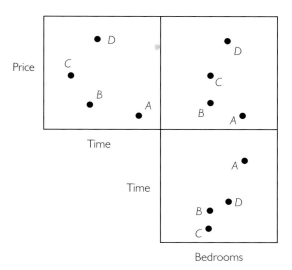

FIGURE 3.14
A scatterplot matrix for the 3D plot of Figure 3.12

to 6*N* while for six variables we have 15*N*. Additionally, the labeling of points can often be impossible in view of the number of points and the screen space available. Fortunately the technique of brushing can aid interpretation. For the scatterplot matrix of Figure 3.14 it is possible to identify a group of points in one of the scatterplots (Figure 3.15) whereupon those objects are highlighted in some way in all the other scatterplots. In this way the effect of one parameter on the relation between the other two can readily be explored. Brushing is particularly useful for hypervariate data, as we shall see later in the book. It is a particular example of subsetting (that is the selection of subsets) which finds wide application. Recently the brushing concept, illustrated here in the context of data, has been extended to the brushing of structure (Fua *et al.*, 1999).

The difficulty associated with the interpretation of Figure 3.12 is also experienced with surfaces such as the example of Figure 3.16. What, for example, is

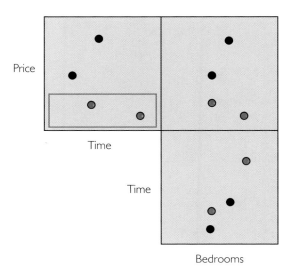

FIGURE 3.15
Brushed points are highlighted on all plots

FIGURE 3.16
A surface in 3D space

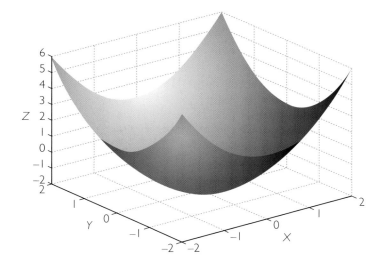

the minimum value of Z? An answer to this and similar questions can be obtained if the viewpoint can be adjusted (Figure 3.17) and if we can use techniques such as 'flooding' (Figure 3.18). A more general approach, reflecting the comment (relevant to Figures 3.12 and 3.16) that 'for 3D to be useful, you've got to move it', is embodied in the spinplot (Fisherkeller *et al.*, 1974). With this tool, the view of a three-dimensional arrangement of points, or a surface, can be freely, easily and continuously adjusted by a user (Figure 3.19(a) and (b)).

As remarked earlier, when the number of dimensions is three it may be appropriate to consider techniques that have been invented to support the visualization of hypervariate data, a topic discussed in the following section. Also, for *any* number of dimensions, techniques such as animation, described in Chapter 2 in the context of sensitivity circles, can often be exploited to 'add another dimension'. If they are, however, one must be aware of any danger asso-

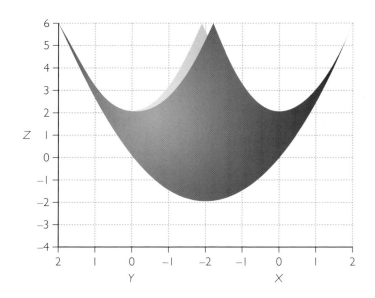

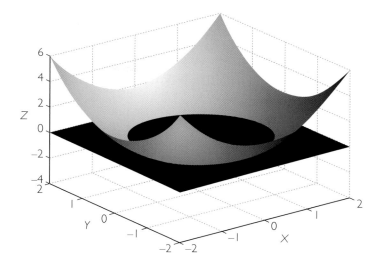

FIGURE 3.18
The technique of 'flooding'

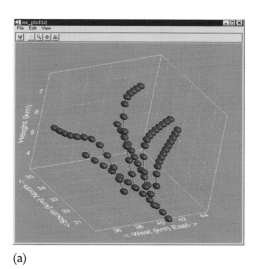

(a)

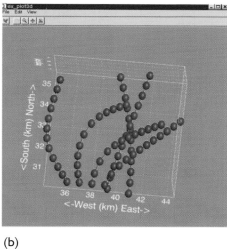

(b)

FIGURE 3.19
A spinplot allows viewing in any direction
Source: *Images produced by IDL, and reproduced by permission*

ciated with the fact that all dimensions may not be given equal perceptual weight: in some applications (see the Influence Explorer, p.160 in Chapter 9) it is important that the display should not be biased to favor the user's view, interpretation or control of a particular variable.

3.7 Hypervariate data

The challenge of visualizing hypervariate (also termed multivariate) data is ongoing, and certainly motivated by the many situations in which the inter-relationships between many variables are of vital interest; engineering design, house-hunting and financial design are just a few of many available examples.

Parallel coordinate plots (Inselberg, 1985, 1998; Wegman, 1990) offer a tried and tested technique which can handle a large number of variables. The principle is simple: it is that of taking all the axes of the multidimensional space and arranging them in order, but parallel to each other. The principle is illustrated in Figure 3.20 with the simple example of two attributes (and hence two parallel coordinates) and two houses (*A* and *C* of Figure 3.13). Essentially, we use that earlier form of presentation (Figure 3.20(a)) but then take the two axes *Price* and *Bedrooms* apart and draw them in parallel (Figure 3.20(b)): each house now appears once on each axis. As it stands, of course, there is nothing to identify which house is which – do we have a cheap house with few bedrooms and an expensive one with more, or an inexpensive house having more bedrooms than the more expensive one? The ambiguity is simply resolved by joining corresponding entries on each scale, as shown in Figure 3.20(c). The two axes are

FIGURE 3.20
The principle of parallel coordinate plots

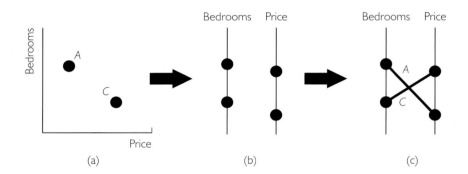

(a)   (b)   (c)

referred to as **parallel coordinates** and the entire presentation as a **parallel coordinate plot**. By reason of its very construction, the concept of parallel coordinates can be extended to any number of variables, as illustrated in Figure 3.21. An example of a parallel coordinate plot relevant to the financial domain is shown in Figure 3.22, where color is used as an additional coding technique. As well as handling quantitative data, parallel coordinate plots can also handle categorical data.

FIGURE 3.21
The principle of parallel coordinate plots applied to six variables

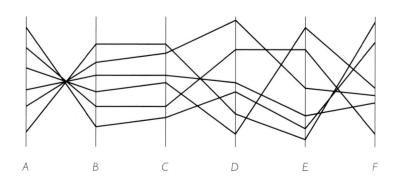

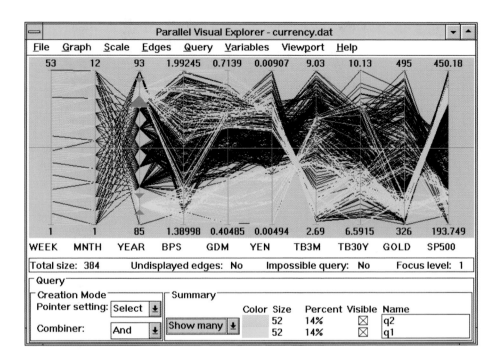

FIGURE 3.22
A parallel coordinate plot for financial variables

Source: *Reproduced by permission from the IBM Corporation*

Certain relationships between variables can easily be deduced from the appearance of the plot. In the simple example of Figure 3.21 there is clearly a trade-off between variables *A* and *B*, and a strong correlation between *B* and *C*, though it has to be said that ease of interpretation can be strongly influenced by the ordering of the axes. However, experts in the interpretation of parallel coordinate plots can derive a great deal of understanding from these plots. Inselberg (1998), for example, provides an interesting illustration related to the enhancement of the manufacturing yield of a process making silicon chips, showing the considerable amount of useful information that can be deduced. More recently, Inselberg and Avidan (1999) have introduced automation to facilitate the elicitation of knowledge from parallel coordinate plots. A significant advantage of parallel coordinate plots, shared by some other visualization tools, is that all variables are treated equally.

The mosaic plot, used in the previous chapter to illustrate the potential of rearrangement, is a useful technique for handling high-dimensional data. If we were to return to the example in Chapter 2 and imagine that the person recording the hair and eye colours of the 592 students also recorded gender, the mosaic plot of Figure 2.9, repeated here as Figure 3.23(a), could be modified as shown in Figure 3.23(b). An extension to even higher dimensionality is illustrated by the Titanic disaster of April 1912, when 1731 of the 2201 passengers and crew were lost (Dawson, 1995). Table 3.2 shows the raw data, involving four variables: *Gender*, *Survival*, *Class* and *Adult/Child*. A number of mosaic plots can be generated (Friendly, 1994), and appropriately interpreted: that shown in Figure 3.24 involves all four attributes.

FIGURE 3.23
(a) The Mosiac
Plot of Figure
2.9 for hair and
eye colours
(b) Modification
of the Mosaic
Plot to include
gender data

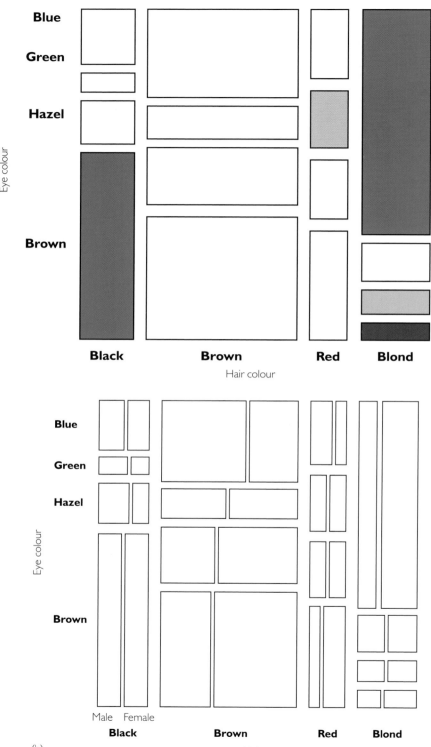

(b)

TABLE 3.2   Data concerning the Titanic disaster

| Survived | Age | Gender | Class | | | |
			1st	2nd	3rd	Crew
No	Adult	Male	118	154	387	670
Yes			57	14	75	192
No	Child		0	0	35	0
Yes			5	11	13	0
No	Adult	Female	4	13	89	3
Yes			140	80	76	20
No	Child		0	0	17	0
Yes			1	13	14	0

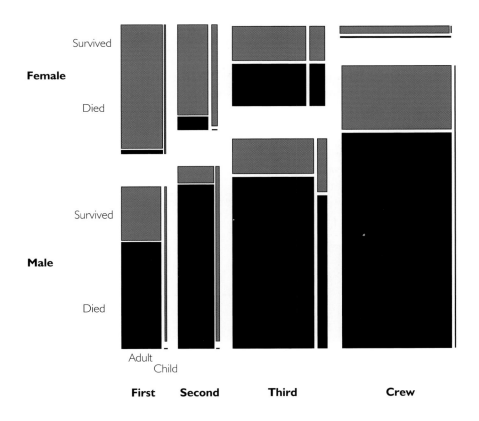

FIGURE 3.24
A Mosaic Plot
for the Titanic
data of Table
3.2

A longstanding means of presenting hypervariate data, and which has much in common with the parallel coordinate plot, is the starplot in which the axes radiate in a star shape from a common origin (Figure 3.25). Thus, a number of objects, each represented by a star plot, might be compared, at least qualitatively, on the basis of their shapes. Alternatively, as with the parallel coordinates, a number of objects can be represented on the same star plot.

FIGURE 3.25
A starplot for eight variables

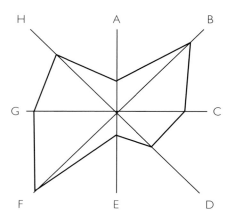

The **hyperbox** (Alpern and Carter, 1991) has the appearance (Figure 3.26) of a solid three-dimensional object, but is so constructed that all possible pairs of variables are shown plotted against each other. Conceptually there is no limit to the number of dimensions that can be handled. One useful feature, which avoids the ordering problem associated with parallel coordinate plots, is that all combinations of two variables are shown. With modern technology any pair can be brought to the front with Cartesian axes, with all others still visible and providing useful context: brushing facilities could easily be added. The hyperbox has been used to observe the behavior of a computer algorithm.

FIGURE 3.26
A hyperbox handling six variables

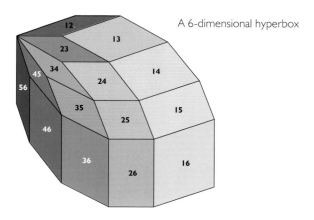

A 6-dimensional hyperbox

3.8 Comment

We have made no comment concerning the intrinsic or relative effectiveness of the various techniques for presenting quantitative data for two reasons. First, because the value of a particular technique depends very much upon the application domain, the user and the task being performed. Second, because a combination of techniques, drawing from this chapter as well as the next, is typically involved in a real world application, and we currently have no way of evaluating the relative merits of techniques combined within a real and usually complex visualization tool of the sort encountered in Chapters 5, 7, 8, 9 and 10. It is for these reasons that we concentrate, in this chapter and the next, on providing a rich palette of techniques from which the visualization tool designer can draw on the basis of judgement and experience.

CHAPTER 4

Representation

4.1 Symbolic encoding

In the previous chapter we addressed the problem of visually representing the **numerical** values associated with an object or an effect, basically by points in a multidimensional space. While there are many circumstances where such representation is appropriate, we need to consider both a wider range of requirements (to be able, for example, to handle **ordinal** and **categorical** data) as well as alternative representations of numerical values appropriate to different circumstances. We have already encountered some examples, including Minard's use of line width for numerical data, Playfair's use of slope and Harry Beck's use of colour to differentiate Underground railway lines (categorical data).

A wide range of symbolic representations are available to encode data (Tufte, 1983, 1990, 1997). Unfortunately there is very little in the way of underlying theory to help us exploit this extensive palette of encoding techniques. As Card *et al.* (1999) remark, 'Innovation is still the overriding activity, generating "point solutions" for theoretical workers to encompass within a general powerful theory'. We shall therefore examine a number of techniques, point to the benefits and disadvantages of each, and provide some idea of the task and environment to which each may be suited.

4.2 Size

An example of the use of size to encode data has already been introduced in Chapter 2. In the MINNIE computer-aided design system (Spence and Apperley, 1977) a circle is superimposed upon components of interest (Figure 4.1), the size of each circle indicating the extent of the influence of that component on a circuit property. Such a symbolic encoding of numerical data is often appropriate in the early stages of design when the designer merely wants to gain a *qualitative* impression of the effect of different components: the designer is concerned, not with whether the sensitivity has a value of 5.2 or 5.3, but rather whether it is small, medium or large, and this is precisely the information that is provided by the circles in Figure 4.1. In the same system boxes appear to indicate (Figure 4.2) the magnitude of the voltage at various points within the circuit: again, precise values may at some stage of design be relevant, whereas a pattern of box sizes could immediately alert the designer to an unexpected situation. As already explained in Chapter 2, an additional dimension, that of frequency, can be displayed by means of an animation in which circle or box sizes take on values appropriate to a displayed frequency (Figure 2.20).

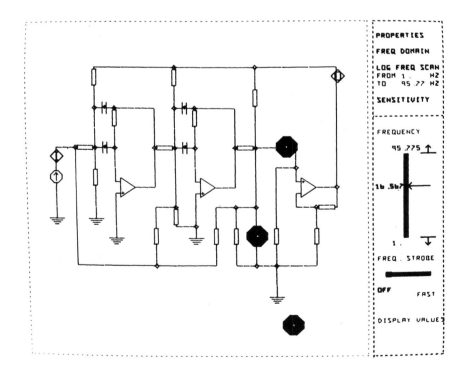

FIGURE 4.1
The size of each circle indicates the effect of the associated component on the performance of the electronic circuit

FIGURE 4.2
Black squares
indicate the
voltage
magnitude at
points within
the circuit

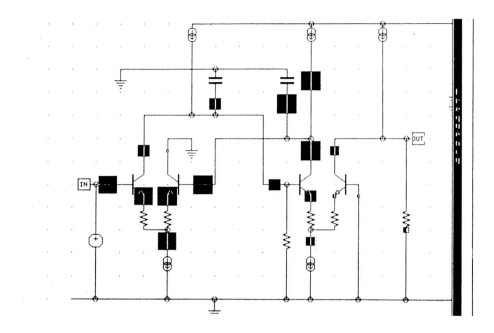

4.3 Length and height

Encoding numerical data by length or height is popular when a qualitative feeling for the data is needed, and can be useful for making comparisons. An example has already been provided by the mosaic plots in the previous two chapters. A different, and more complex example can be found in a system (Colgan *et al.*, 1995) which automatically and quite rapidly changes the values of electrical components in order to improve the design of a circuit. The designer who monitors that process and intervenes when necessary has many representations to interpret within the displayed data (Figure 4.3): apart from component values which are changing quite rapidly – maybe once or twice per second – the designer must observe and interpret a large number of red circles (some of which are seen in Figure 4.3) which together provide a view of the current quality of the design. Under these circumstances a numeric display of component values would be wholly inappropriate, so bar heights are employed, as seen in the lower part of Figure 4.3. The length of each bar indicates the current value chosen for that component by the computer, and the maximum length (indicated by the 'box' containing each bar) represents the limits that the designer has tentatively placed on those components. As automated design proceeds, the bars increase and decrease in height quite rapidly as the computer incrementally improves the circuit. The designer can learn a great deal from observation of the bars: for example, if a bar keeps 'hitting' its upper or lower limit – which will normally have been specified quite tentatively – it is probably wise to extend the limit to see if a marked improvement occurs.

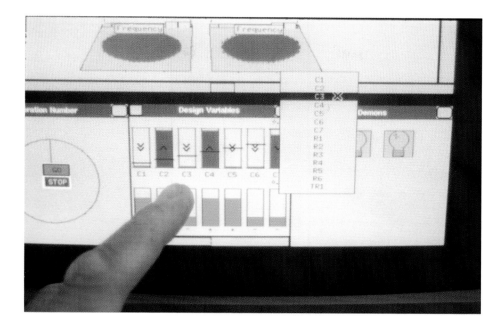

FIGURE 4.3
Part of the 'Cockpit' by means of which a human engineering designer observes the progress of automated design. The red circles indicate the quality of different parts of the design and the top row of bars indicate the current values of the components that are being adjusted automatically

Consideration of the value of bar heights as a means of representation provides an opportunity to discuss two issues: one is the value of *qualitative* representation and interpretation and the other concerns the frequent need for a composite visualization tool which allows a user to switch rapidly between qualitative and quantitative interpretation. As an illustration we select the design (Figure 4.4) of an altimeter for the cockpit of a light aircraft.[1] The vertical bar provides, and is enhanced by familiar colour coding, an easily perceived qualitative indication of aircraft altitude: it is easy to see if one is flying at an acceptable or a dangerous height. Closely located is a quantitative indication of altitude, so that little eye movement is required to change from a qualitative enquiry to a quantitative one. The digital indication is carefully chosen to conform with conventional practice, where altitude is often quoted in hundreds of feet. The last two digits of the digital presentation are, for that reason, chosen to be smaller in size so as to avoid confusion but to provide an unambiguous indication of altitude. Since altitude varies continuously rather than in discrete steps the presentation of the last two digits is also continuous and is so chosen that no ambiguity arises when both those digits are zero. The altimeter design illustrates the fact that, in practice, the designer is faced with combining a variety of representations to handle the tasks that must be supported.

---

[1] I'm grateful to Neil Mothew (a pilot) for this example.

FIGURE 4.4
Design for an
altimeter which
provides both
qualitative and
quantitative
indications of
altitude
Source: *Neil
Motthew, 1999*

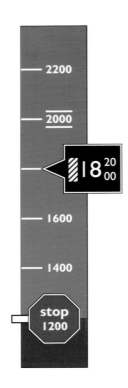

4.4 Magnification

It is possible to employ a human being's well-developed memory of the conventional world atlas to use magnification as an encoding scheme for geographic data. Thus, if the number of bicycles per head of population in New Zealand is ten times that in Australia, then this fact can be encoded in a map (Figure 4.5) in which New Zealand is magnified relative to Australia to reflect the ratio of bicycle ownership. This method of encoding has been extensively and effectively employed in *The New State of the World Atlas* (Smith, 1999). In Figure 4.6, con-

FIGURE 4.5
The use of
magnification to
illustrate
relative bicycle
ownership in
two countries

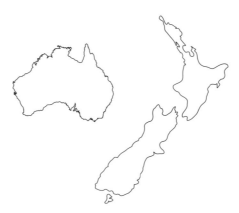

cerned with population, the small size of Canada and Australia is immediately noticeable, as are the comparatively large sizes of India and Japan. Though effective in providing an immediate qualitative impression, use of this encoding mechanism relies heavily upon a good memory for sizes.

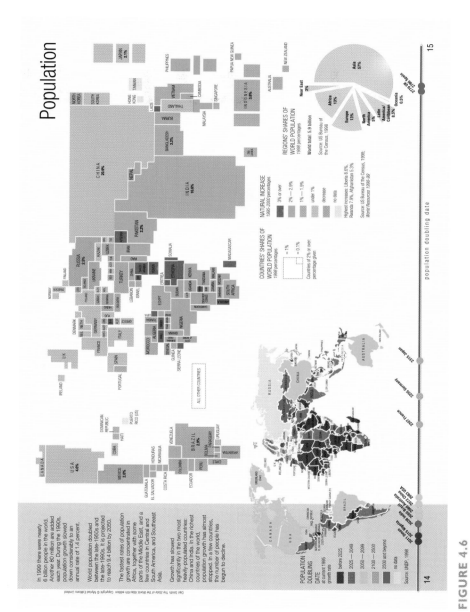

FIGURE 4.6

Area magnification is used to indicate national populations

Source: *Smith (1999)*

4.5 Faces

Professor Herman Chernoff, a statistician at Stanford University, observed that human beings are very sensitive to a wide range of facial expressions and appearance, and suggested that facial features such as the size of the eyes, the height of eyebrows above the eyes and the shape of the mouth are quite numerous and could, in a cartoon face, take on a sufficiently large number of 'values' to offer a useful encoding mechanism (Figure 4.7). He therefore applied this technique (Chernoff, 1973) to the study of geological samples, each characterized by 18 attributes (for example, salt content, water content), and found that the display of so-called Chernoff faces facilitated the identification of interesting groups of samples. If this use of computer-controlled cartoon faces should appear frivolous, it should be remarked that accountants, not perhaps typically known for frivolous behavior, have also explored the use of Chernoff faces to display accountancy data (Stock and Watson, 1984). Studies by De Soete (1986) have established the relative value of the various facial features. Following Chernoff's proposal it was recognized that half a face carries the same information as a full symmetrical face, stimulating studies of asymmetrical faces (Flury and Riedwyl, 1981).

FIGURE 4.7
Chernoff faces, in which facial characteristics encode the values of variables

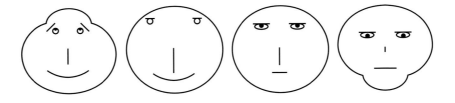

4.6 Multidimensional icons

A Chernoff face is an example of a multidimensional icon: in the example investigated by Chernoff himself the dimensionality was 18. It is not difficult to propose other multidimensional icons appropriate to different tasks and different domains. One example specifically designed to explore the effectiveness of multidimensional icons addressed the problem of selecting, from a number of alternatives, a house satisfying certain requirements (Spence and Parr, 1991). Sample icons are shown in Figure 4.8: colour encodes a price band (red is over £400,000, orange between £300,000 and £400,000, yellow between £200,000 and £300,000 and white between £100,000 and £200,000) while shape encodes a categorical variable (house, houseboat, flat, and cottage). The number of bedrooms was indicated by the number of windows, and these were coloured black or white to denote, respectively, a bad or good state of repair. Garden size was indicated by size, the presence of a garage and central heating each by a symbol and journey time by a clock segment. Overall, eight dimensions are represented.

 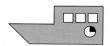

house	Flat	houseboat
£400,000	£300,000	£200,000
garage	no garage	no garage
central heating	central heating	no central heating
four bedrooms	two bedrooms	three bedrooms
good repair	poor repair	good repair
large garden	small garden	no garden
Victoria 15 mins	Victoria 20 mins	Victoria 15 mins

FIGURE 4.9
Textual presentation of the same data encoded in Figure 4.8

Controlled experiments were undertaken to investigate any advantage such icons might offer over a simple textual description of the form shown in Figure 4.9. Typically, a subject was given the following task:

> *You can spend up to £200,000 on accommodation. Locate the best you can with regard to the number of bedrooms and the size of garden, but it must have central heating.*

Overall, it was found that the time taken to identify the appropriate house using icons was about half what it was using a textual description. It was suggested that one significant advantage of the icons was their semantic relation to the task, a relation not present when using faces, for example, to represent geological samples.

4.7 Spatiality

Alistair Cooke, the author for more than 40 years of the BBC radio program *Letter from America*, had the problem of storing his vast collection of books about the American states. Many people would have chosen an alphabetical ordering. Instead, Cooke (1973) relied on his excellent knowledge of the geographical location of the American states and used that 'mental map' as the basis for distributing his books around the bookshelves. Thus, books about Florida were to be found on the lowest shelf at the right, whereas those about California were at waist height at the left-hand end. It is not recorded where books on Hawaii were stored – perhaps on a table to the left of the bookshelves!

Cooke's solution exploits the human being's excellent spatial memory, a characteristic that can be exploited in many ways. Malone (1983), for example, remarked upon how an office worker creates piles of documents on a desk to signify that they need attention, and how different piles have different significance. The spatial characteristics and visual appearance of the piles constitute the externalization of attributes: the user's internal model is continually reinforced by the action of placing a document on a pile and creating new piles.

The relevance of spatial memory to visualization is clear. Since visualization is the creation and enhancement of an internal model, it is useful to know that spatiality as a basis appears to lead to a robust internal model, and therefore that phenomena having no inherent location could perhaps be assigned an artificial location – consistently used throughout – in order to enhance the likelihood of a robust internal model.

4.8 Patterns

Patterns can provide a valuable approach to encoding, especially when combined with other encoding techniques. The patterns shown in Figure 4.10(a) and (b) appear in a visualization tool adopted by a large company to investigate and help diagnose problems occurring in the manufacture of mass-produced domestic equipment.[2] The pattern is formed in three dimensional space in which the 'horizontal' plane has axes associated with month of production (MOP) and months in service (MIS). Plotted vertically is the failure rate. In Figure 4.10(a) the pattern indicates an epidemical failure. Other characteristic failure patterns that can occur, and their interpretation, are shown in Figure 4.10(b). Area 2, for example, occurs exactly twelve months after manufacture, corresponding to the end of the guarantee period; area 7 corresponds to an epidemical failure associated with one particular month's production, and area 4 refers to latent defects. By examining such patterns the investigator can draw conclusions about the production process as it proceeds.

Another field in which human pattern recognition can be useful is that of social intercourse. Although social interaction via the Internet is becoming common through the use of online 'chat environments', present-day embodiments leave much to be desired. The associated display (Figure 4.11) suffers from many constraints with regard to the social cues that can be made explicit. Thus, anyone not messaging (but possibly 'listening') does not appear in the summary; a participant may therefore feel compelled to post a message simply to establish a presence; there is a cost in having repeatedly to read the names of participants; and the conversational dynamics are not explicit. Many of these drawbacks are removed, and other benefits accrue, from a recently invented graphical interface (Figure 4.12) called Chat Circles (Viegas and Donath, 1999) which allows dialogs to be visualized. Here, where time proceeds downwards, coloured circles represent a participant (contributory or otherwise), the colour being used as a discriminant rather than as an identifier,[3] the latter function being supplied by a label containing the participant's name. The size of the circle expands, and is immediately noticed, as a message is posted; the message appears within the circle and the colour of the circle

---

[2] I'm very grateful to Harald Noordweijk for drawing my attention to this example and supplying the figure from his thesis.

[3] The use of colour to enable a user to discriminate between participants poses some difficulty. The colour red, for example, is a sign of danger in the West but is interpreted as good luck in China.

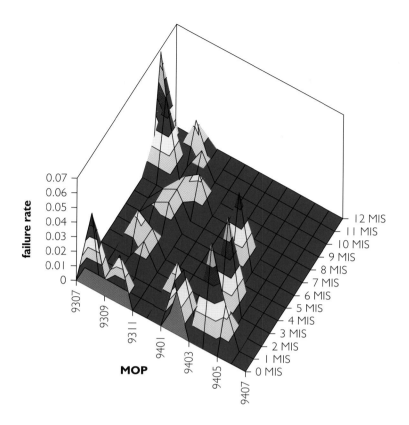

FIGURE 4.10
(a) Failure rate of a manufactured artefact is plotted against month of production and month in service
(b) Characteristic patterns that can occur, and their interpretation

Source: *Harold Noordhoek*

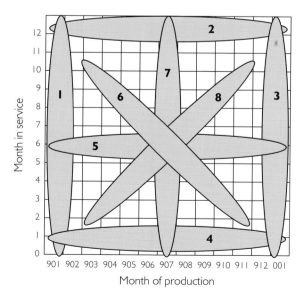

1 running in production
2 end of guarantee period
3 running out production
4 latent defects
5 early wearout, creep, aging
6 season influence
7 epidemical failure
8 learning curve

\<le_beau\> where can i find wvdial
\<The_Vox\> le_beau: freshmeat.net
\<le_beau\> ok thanx!
\<The_Vox\> np
***le_beau has left #linuxhelp
\<W0w08\> hello
\<DA9L\> is there any external win modems
\<D-side\> Yo
*** knowbody_has joined #linuxhelp
\<{Q-Ball}\> The_Vox: thanks

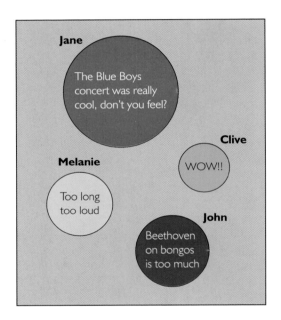

brightens. After the message has been posted the circle gradually decreases in size. As the inventors point out, 'The resulting graphical cadence becomes an important articulator of the flow of conversation . . .'. Other parameters of the display encode additional valuable information: proximity of circles is related, for example, to whether or not a person can hear a particular conversation.

A related tool supports the visualization of an archive of a conversation. In the display of Figure 4.13, in which time again proceeds downwards, a colour-coded vertical line is associated with each conversational participant, and horizontal bars represent utterances. In this simple representation – a sort of conversational landscape – we see that person *C* is a 'lurker', constantly listening but not contributing, whereas contributor *A* is dominant. Logical zooming allows the actual conversion to be monitored.

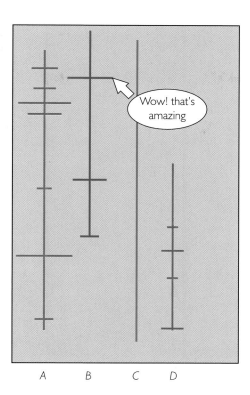

FIGURE 4.13
An archive of a
conversation
carried out by
Chat Circles

4.9 Software engineering

The design, development and evaluation of software is, like any other branch of engineering, a task of great complexity in which success is enhanced by the ability of the designer to develop relevant models of that software's behavior under various conditions and at different stages of development. It is for this reason that tools are available that can provide statistics regarding, for each line of code, such aspects as authorship, date of last change, purpose of last change (bug fix or new functionality), how it is reached, how often it is executed, and so on. Nevertheless, the sheer volume of code (perhaps thousands or millions of lines) is such that it is not easy to gain insight or obtain a global view of the software from these statistics. Fortunately, the techniques of information visualization can help immensely, especially when integrated within a well-designed tool. Seesoft (Eick *et al.*, 1992) is one such tool.

Seesoft embodies three information visualization techniques which are illustrated in Figure 4.14. This figure shows the representation of a directory comprising twenty source code files containing a total of 9365 lines of code. Files are represented as columns, and individual lines of code by thin rows. The colour of each line shows that line's age: the scale used is the rainbow scale with the newest lines in red and the oldest in blue. Rows are just large enough so that block comments, functions and control structures (for example, *if* and *case*) are visible merely by their indentation.

FIGURE 4.14
The
representation
of a directory
containing 20
source code
files

Source: © 1992
IEEE

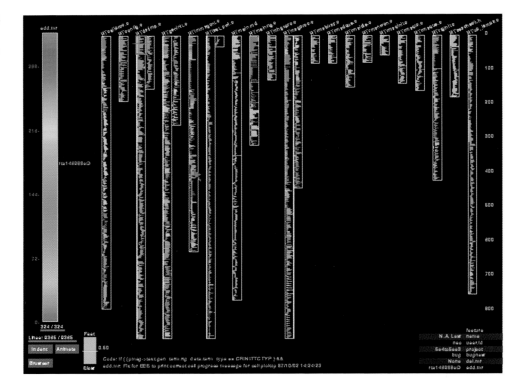

4.10 Sound

In one sense it is unfortunate that the term 'visualization' contains the term 'visual', since an aural presentation of data – on its own or combined with visual presentation – has much to offer. Classical concert-goers and rock band enthusiasts alike are capable of identifying not only the different musical instruments, of which there may be twenty or more, but also the different notes, chords, tempo, and rhythm that are being played, so the potential for encoding data in sound appears considerable. Aural presentation also possesses some features that are not present in visual presentations. As Card *et al.* (1999) remark, 'The capacity to pick up outliers, akin to the missed note in a symphony performance, may be greater in sonic environments'. As they additionally point out, auditory information is omnidirectional and can easily be heard when not being attended to, and they illustrate this property by describing the playing, through a loudspeaker, of the sound of laboratory results, allowing staff to move around freely. Indeed, when using an automatic teller machine, we are now used to hearing a 'beep' to indicate a change of state of the machine, a very simple but extremely effective way of encoding data in sound and thereby allowing the state of the machine to be visualized.

Figure 4.15 refers to the use of audio encoding in the study of a brain tumour. What is seen in that figure is the result of an MRI scan of a brain, with a tumour clearly visible (Grinstein, 1999). However, the clinical investigator can also point to a particular part of the brain scan and deduce, from the continuous sound that is triggered, some aspect of that tumour.

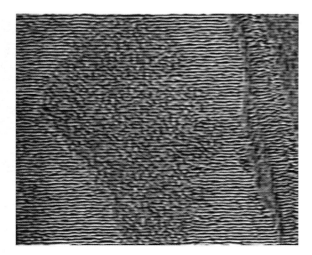

FIGURE 4.15
Visual presentation of a brain tumour whose details can additionally be visualized by sound triggered by the location of a cursor

Source: *Grinstein (1999)*

4.11   Virtual worlds

One is aware, when viewing a Web page, that thousands of other people may concurrently be viewing the same page; nevertheless, one has no way of knowing. A more striking realization, however, is that social interaction with them is impossible: there is no opportunity to ask them about the content being viewed; there is no opportunity to meet someone with similar interests. To overcome these severe constraints, research is currently underway into electronic imaginary worlds ('virtual worlds'), rendered in three dimensions, with shared user access over a network. In such a world people can explore, socialise, acquire information, teach, play, and generally do most things possible in the real world (Rankin *et al*., 1998).

The concept of virtual worlds identifies many visualization issues. One is that of representing the user within the virtual world. One approach, of course, is to employ a representation resembling, as closely as possible, the actual appearance of the user. But for many reasons, such as privacy, a symbolic representation may be preferred. One example is called the StarCursor (Rankin *et al*, 1998) and has the general appearance illustrated in Figure 4.16.

The anthropomorphic StarCursor is characterized graphically by rudimentary heart, body, limbs, eye, and aura: all of these are multimedia channels for personal disclosures, communicative signals and actions. A person's interests filter what they see about other cursors: personal data about medical history, hobbies and current mood can be made available at the discretion of the 'owner' of a cursor. Within the huge range of research questions raised by such a facility, however, we concentrate – perhaps cursorily in view of the many issues involved – on some parameters of the personal cursor. The body, for example, provides an opportunity for 'clothing' to reflect mood (as in real life), body shape can indicate attitude, and the aura (both visible and audible) can indicate interest or mood. One might hesitate to approach the group shown in Figure 4.17, but feel quite uninhibited about making contact with the group depicted in Figure 4.18.

FIGURE 4.16
A StarCursor
representing a
human being in
a virtual world

Source: *StarCursor
Design © Philips
Electronics N.V.
1998. Reproduced
with permission.*

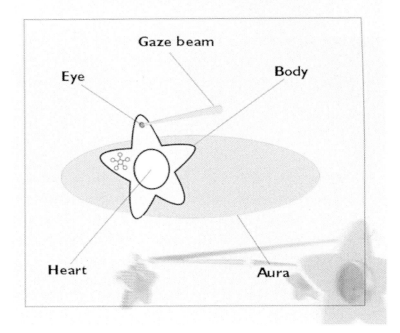

FIGURE 4.17
A group of
inhospitable
StarCursors

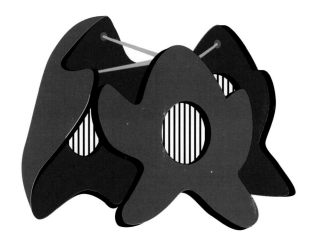

4.12 Colour

As already demonstrated, numerical data can be encoded by colour. Use of
colour should be undertaken with caution, however, and not with the hysterical
abandon of a child discovering its first paint box. There is, for example, a minimum size of line or point whose colour can easily be discriminated, and a

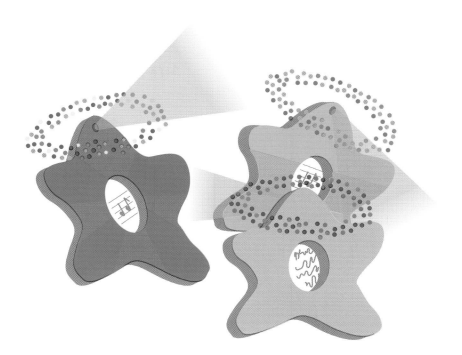

FIGURE 4.18
A group of
welcoming
StarCursors

consequent need to exercise care in the construction of graphs. Colour scales to represent magnitude should also be chosen carefully. A popular choice is the spectrum, with red denoting large elements and blue the small elements. Another was mentioned in Section 4.6 in connection with encoding the price ranges of houses for sale. Here, the scale red–orange–yellow–white was employed to denote decreasing values, and it is interesting to note that, during the associated experiments, none of the hundred or so subjects asked to be reminded about this scheme. An alternative familiar from geographic atlases is the green, light green, light brown, dark brown, gray, and white sequence. Grayscale shading (Figure 4.19) can also be used to advantage, though there is quite a low limit to the number of shades that can satisfactorily be discriminated. There are many other guidelines to the use of colour (Jackson *et al.*, 1994). A good illustration of the use of both colour coding and animation is provided by the GVis ('geographical visualization') system (MacEachren *et al.*, 1998) as shown in Figures 4.20 and 4.21. It also illustrates a parallel with the electronic circuit example discussed in Section 4.2 in that spatial layout is meaningful: the investigator using GVis is aware of the layout of American states just as the circuit designer knows where each component is located as well as its anticipated effect on circuit performance. The display of Figure 4.20 is concerned with georeferenced health statistics: it uses the colour ordering dark purple, medium purple, light purple, grey, light green, medium green, dark green

FIGURE 4.19
Encoding by
grayscale
shading

FIGURE 4.20
Illustration of
the use of
colour in the
display of
georeferenced
health statistics
Source: *MacEachren*

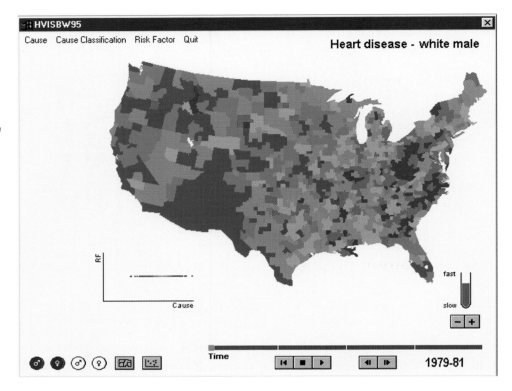

FIGURE 4.21
A bivariate
cross map,
illustrating the
benefits of
interactive
rearrangment

Source: *MacEachren*

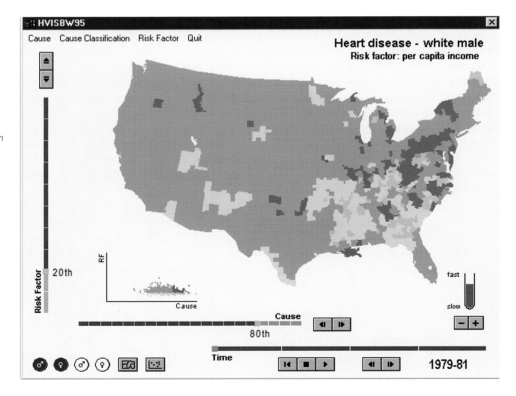

to depict white male, age-adjusted, heart disease mortality rates by health service area (HSA) over the period 1979–1981. The colour scheme puts emphasis on the two extremes and on the middle of the range. At the lower edge of the display, familiar video controls facilitate automated animation of an adjustable speed along a 'time line', though direct manipulation is also supported.

The benefit of interactive rearrangement, discussed in Chapter 2, is illustrated in the bivariate cross map of Figure 4.21: it depicts white male, age-adjusted, heart disease mortality rates in the period 1979–81 crossed with per capita income. Both of these variables are focused on the 80th percentile. Blue represents HSAs with a mortality rate in the top 20 per cent, and light shades depict income in the lower 80 per cent with a few dark blues depicting the anomalous high-income–high death-rate HSAs. In this way light blue indicates HSAs with a high rate of heart disease and low income. Characteristics of expert use of the GVis system are discussed by MacEachren *et al.* (1998).

4.13   Comment

Exposure to the many ways of encoding data visually and aurally prompts the obvious question 'Which is best?' In one sense the answer is 'it depends', since the task for which the user seeks to form a mental model can take many different forms, and the domain for which the data is encoded can also vary widely. In another sense the answer is 'we don't know'. Various attempts have been made to identify, separately for numeric, categorical and ordinal data, the comparative benefits of a variety of encoding techniques such as length, size, angle and colour. Cleveland and McGill (1984), for example, presented working hypotheses about this issue, as did Mackinlay (1986) with a view to automating the design of visualization tools. Nevertheless, the fact remains that the issue is still unresolved. Contributory factors to this lack of knowledge include the fact that encoding techniques are rarely used in isolation, that the task itself influences the best choice of encoding, that a real visualization tool is normally quite complex and must satisfy a number of constraints, and that early assessments of encoding techniques concentrated on passive and some active visualization tools rather than on the more recent dynamic tools. It is for this reason that the approach of this and the previous chapter has been to present a rich palette of techniques whose application in a wide range of tools is illustrated in the remaining chapters.

Dynamic Exploration

5.1 Real problems

When someone has a problem to solve it may not be clearly formulated, either consciously or unconsciously. The house-hunter[1] may wish to '*try* to keep the cost below *about* £100,000, *try* for 3 bedrooms (but 4 would be *nice*), see if we can find something near a *good* school and, perhaps, *close* to Granny who might baby-sit for us'. As emphasized by the italics, the word 'precision' does not leap to mind. Nevertheless, a great many problems are often just as imprecisely articulated at first, and for good reason.

That reason is a lack of knowledge. The house-hunter does not know what houses are currently on the market, is possibly a stranger to the locality where a house is needed, and may have no idea whatsoever of the general level of prices. The first task, therefore, is to help the house-hunter to gain an understanding, not only of the relevant data, but additionally of any 'hidden' relationships such as a steep increase in price as one nears Pearson's Park. The next task is to empower them to solve their problem, that of finding a satisfactory house. Often, in the course of acquiring knowledge about available houses, the requirements may be modified ('looks like we *could* afford a 5-bedroom house if we

---

[1] Ideally, we should use the term 'home-hunting' to describe the process of looking for a new house, since it is the environment (a nearby park, graffiti on the walls, proximity to a good school), as well as the physical house, that will influence the selection of a particular house to buy. For simplicity we use the term 'house-hunting' throughout.

70

take in paying guests'). Thus, in practice, problem formulation is often equally as important as problem solution, and the two can usefully proceed together using, as they do, the same data. What is especially valuable to the person with a problem to solve is a means of visualizing the relevant data in such a way as to support these two activities, as well as a smooth transition between them.

To identify issues, and thereby help to establish guidelines and criteria for the application of visualization techniques, we first examine – perhaps paradoxically – a dated, textual command-based query system.

5.2 Command line query

With a conventional database query language the house-hunter might be expected to enter a query of the form:

> **Select** house-address
> **From** mydatabase
> **Where** price < = 100,000 **and**
> Bathrooms = 2 **and**
> Bedrooms >= 3

to indicate that the most that can be afforded is £100,000, that two bathrooms are essential (no more, no less) and that the house should have at least three bedrooms. The result, of course, could be:

0 HITS

indicating that the estate agent can offer no houses satisfying these requirements. Equally unhelpful can be the response:

1328 HITS

especially if there is no indication as to how the query might usefully be modified. How much more or less should I offer?

There are, in fact, many disadvantages associated with conventional database query languages, and it is useful to identify them. Here are seven:

1. The discretionary user must learn a language. Except for specialist users, people are not prepared to do this. Even for query languages claimed to be simple (for example, Query by Example), controlled tests have shown that even after about an hour's tutelage insufficient familiarity was acquired (Borgman, 1986).[2]

---

[2] Borgman (1986) found that after a day's instruction only a quarter of the Stanford University students she tested could use the library's online query system. Additionally she found that users tend to make very simple queries and not use the full complexity of Boolean expressions.

2. Errors are not tolerated. Users are now becoming familiar with systems which do not permit syntactical errors, and would expect such a feature in any new tool.

3. Too few or too many 'hits' may occur. This is not surprising if the user has little or no knowledge of the database.

4. If there are too few or too many hits, there is no indication of how the query might beneficially be reformulated. By paying an extra £500 the 'house of my dreams' might be available: I would certainly want to be made aware of this.

5. There is a significant time delay between the formulation of a new query and the delivery of its result. There are two principal reasons. First, the user must formulate a new query in their mind. Second, they must enter it without error. A third possible reason may be an inherent delay in processing the entered query. Any delay discourages a 'let's see if . . .' approach which can efficiently lead to the acquisition of insight into the data being explored.

6. Useful contextual data is unnecessarily hidden. The importance of context – of a global model within which a local solution is to be found – has already been emphasized (see item 4 above).

7. As a result of all these drawbacks, it can be difficult for the user to build an internal model or cognitive map of the data, which is what information visualization is all about.

Behind all these drawbacks is the very basis on which a typical command-line query language is grounded: an assumption that a user knows precisely what single question needs to be asked and, additionally, knows a great deal about the database. The rejection of this assumption is fundamental to the developments we now describe. We first concentrate on the need to formulate a problem, and hence the need to acquire, by visualization, some idea of the content and characteristics of the database. What will permeate this chapter is the effectiveness of exploration – and in particular *dynamic exploration* – in gaining some qualitative idea of the database content while moving towards a satisfactory solution.

5.3 Dynamic queries

Perhaps the most significant recent acknowledgement of the fact that a user formulates a problem concurrently with solving it was the concept of dynamic queries, first reported by Williamson and Shneiderman (1992). An effective illustration (Figure 5.1) is again provided by a lay person's search for a house. To the right of a map are scales with adjustable sliding limits, each associated with a particular attribute of a house: *Price,* number of *Bedrooms* and *Journey time* to work are typical examples. Adjustment of the upper and/or lower acceptable limits to any of these attributes causes the corresponding selection to be made from all houses in the database, and the result of that selection immediately displayed by dots on the map. A significant advantage is that *responsive interaction*, by which we mean that an effect occurs within less than about 0.1 seconds of its cause, not only allows answers to be obtained rapidly but, most importantly, supports

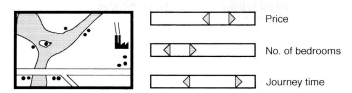

FIGURE 5.1
The dynamic
homefinder

dynamic exploration, often called the 'what if . . .?' activity. Even though no direct indication of how a query might usefully be modified is given, some indication can now be obtained manually by exploratory variation of the attribute limits: any advantage of paying £500 more is immediately indicated by the appearance of another dot on the map. The dynamic query technique, in fact, overcomes most of the seven drawbacks identified in the previous section.

Since the task to which the dynamic homefinder is addressed will be referred to again, it is useful to state it in generic terms:

> *Given a collection of objects, each described by the values associated with a set of attributes, find the most acceptable such object or, perhaps, a small number of candidate objects worthy of more detailed consideration.*

5.3.1 To find a film

The same type of task is involved in the selection of a film to watch on video, for which the Spotfire display of Figure 5.2(a) is relevant (Ahlberg and Shneiderman, 1994). On the main display each coloured square identifies a film. Colour represents type (horror, musical, etc.), horizontal position indicates the year of production and vertical position indicates duration. On the right, sliders can be used to specify other attributes such as type, director, actor and other characteristics of a film. Scroll bars can be used to confine attention to a particular span of years and film length, allowing more detail to be displayed and explored (Figure 5.2(b)).

The visualization tool shown in Figure 5.2 also contains an effective way of compactly making a selection from a particular class of menu, called alphasliders (Figure 5.3). The alphaslider technique, first proposed by Osada *et al.* (1993), and described in detail by Ahlberg (1996) allows users to scan rapidly through, and select items from, lists of alphabetic data. The essential components of the alphaslider shown in Figure 5.3 are a slide area, a slider thumb, a text output and, running underneath the slider, an index of the elements over which the slider operates. Guided by the user's view of the index and knowledge of the required initial letter, a mouse-click on the slider causes the thumb to move appropriately and the selected text item to appear. In Figure 5.3 the user, wishing to examine film titles beginning with 'H' has clicked the slide area just above the 'H' displayed in the index, whereupon the thumb has repositioned and the output 'Hunt for Red October' has appeared. If this title was not the one sought, gentle direct manipulation (for example, by mouse drag) of the thumb allows exploration. Not all the letters of the alphabet need appear in the index: a combination of the most popular and a reasonable spread could be best. An improved alphaslider shown in Figure 5.4 allows a choice of fine and coarse tuning.

FIGURE 5.2
Dynamic
queries applied
to the selection
of a film. Detail
can be
disclosed

Source: *Spotfire AB*

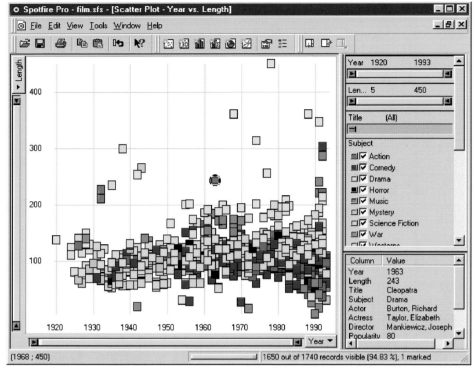

(a)

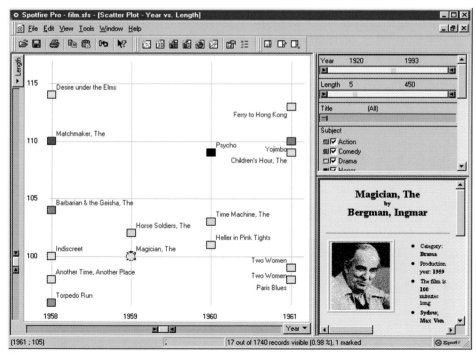

(b)

FIGURE 5.3
An alphaslider

FIGURE 5.4
An improved
alphaslider

5.3.2 Discovery

The dynamic queries concept has more general application than finding one or
more desirable objects within a group. The illustration of Figure 5.5, for example, relates to demographic studies of Sweden, and in particular to the
distribution of pollutants. Control panels on the right-hand side of the display
allow the selection of the year involved (1975 and 1985 in the illustration) and,

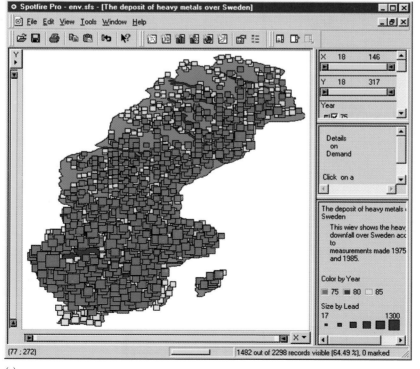

FIGURE 5.5 (a)
A display of
heavy metal
deposits in
Sweden

Source: *Spotfire AB*

(a)

FIGURE 5.5 (b)

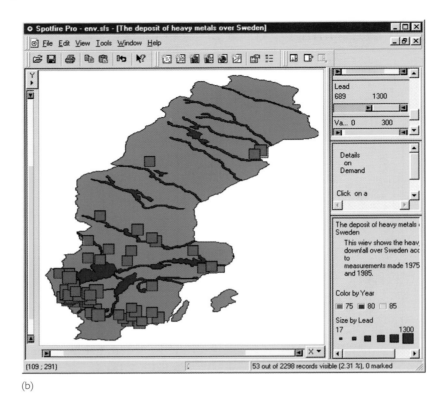

(b)

via the sliders, the thresholds above which a given heavy metal is to be displayed on the map. It is not difficult to appreciate that the technique of dynamic queries can support discovery and the formulation of hypotheses leading to a rearrangement of relevant data (Figure 5.5(b)).

5.3.3 Insensitivity

An interesting feature (Figure 5.6) can be associated with the sliders in Figure 5.5. Within each slider, a gray area indicates that range within which no objects are to be found as a result of other limits placed on other attributes. Thus, if a limit placed on *Price* is such that all 1-, 2- and 3-bedroom houses are thereby excluded, then this fact is registered on the *Bedrooms* scale, as shown in Figure 5.6. It follows that the selection is now insensitive to movement of the lower limit on *Bedrooms* as far up as 4 bedrooms. Such information can be of considerable value to the user.

FIGURE 5.6
An alphaslider feature indicating insensitivity to limit variation

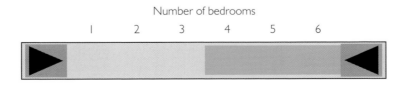

5.4 The Attribute Explorer

A drawback to the dynamic queries concept as proposed by Williamson and Shneiderman (1992) is that data is disclosed only when it satisfies the query. In other words, only those objects are identified whose attribute values satisfy all limits. At first this sounds reasonable, especially in those cases where the display would otherwise be crowded. Nevertheless, as we shall now show, there are situations in which the display of *all* data provides **contextual information** yielding extremely valuable guidance for exploration.

To illustrate the value of contextual information we return to the house-hunting scenario where there is a (usually large) collection of objects, each described by a number of attributes, and where the task is that which was stated earlier:

> *Given a collection of objects, each described by the values associated with a set of attributes, find the most acceptable such object or, perhaps, a small number of candidate objects worthy of more detailed consideration.*

As originally pointed out in Chapter 3, the data associated with an attribute can conveniently be displayed (Figure 5.7) in the form of a histogram composed of rectangles, each associated with one of the houses in the collection. A mouse-hit on the histogram can reveal, as shown in the figure, the value of the attribute for that house. Below the histogram is a scale whose extremities indicate the range of attribute values associated with the objects. Located on the scale are two limits which can be adjusted interactively (Figure 5.8) to specify a range of acceptable attribute values, and hence a subset of the collection of objects. This subset can be encoded with colour, as shown in Figure 5.8. It is, nevertheless, often valuable – as in Figure 5.8 – to retain the (white) display of the unselected objects since, as will soon be apparent, they provide valuable contextual information.

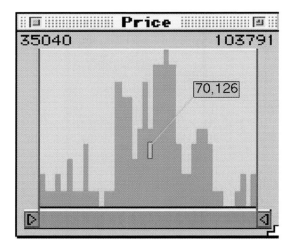

FIGURE 5.7
A histogram of house prices

FIGURE 5.8
Placement of
lower and
upper limits to
identify a set of
houses

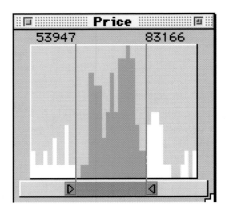

Usually, many attributes will be of concern to the user, but in the interests of space we shall consider only three: *Price*, number of *Bedrooms* and *Garden size*. Figure 5.9 shows the corresponding attribute histograms, but with the same limits on *Price* as in Figure 5.8. Each house appears once on each histogram. The effect shown is that of 'brushing' discussed in Chapter 3, in that the objects selected according to the *Price* limits are encoded green not only in the *Price* histogram but additionally in the remaining histograms. Such linking between histograms now allows the interrelation between the three attributes to be easily explored. It is for this reason that a set of interactive linked attribute histograms such as that of Figure 5.9 is called the Attribute Explorer (Spence and Tweedie, 1998).

FIGURE 5.9
A selected Price
range is
brushed over
the Bedrooms
and Garden
Size histograms

A rapid way of gaining initial insight into the interrelations is to use the fact that the 'bar' between the limits on each attribute scale can itself be located manually (Figure 5.10): a quick movement of the *Price* bar up and down the scale, for example, and simultaneous observation of the green components on the other two histograms, might reveal that cheaper houses tend to have smaller gardens (but perhaps, at the same time, indicate interesting exceptions such as cheap houses with large gardens).

What makes the Attribute Explorer especially valuable is the fact that the set of objects encoded by colour on all the histograms can be determined by limits placed on *all* attribute values, as shown in Figure 5.11, making it possible for a

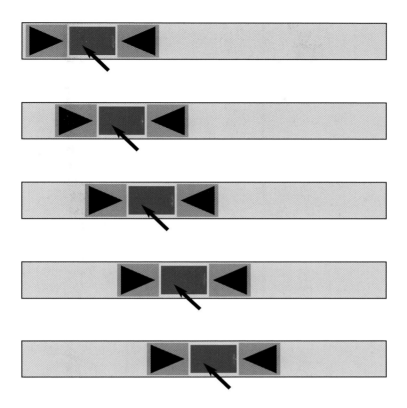

FIGURE 5.10
A bar on a histogram scale can be moved as a single entity

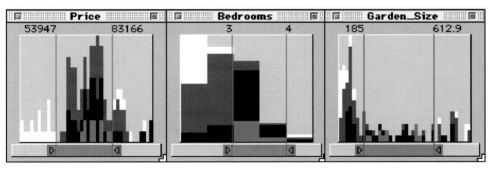

FIGURE 5.11
In the Attribute Explorer separate limits on three attributes combine to identify houses that satisfy all limits

user to explore the interrelations between attributes very thoroughly.[3] Stated formally, the object selection shown in green is the result of performing a Boolean AND operation on the objects identified by the separate attribute ranges. Figure 5.12 provides a reminder that latitude and longitude form an interesting pair of attributes that can be handled together, allowing the user to

---

[3] The colour-coded rectangles representing houses in the histogram are continuously 'lower justified', for the following reason. If a limit on *Price* is changed it may render unacceptable a house in the *Bedrooms* histogram, represented perhaps by a rectangle below which there are acceptable houses. Such a change is difficult to follow, so it is arranged that in all columns of all histograms the ordering (starting at the bottom) is green, black, dark gray, light gray and so on.

FIGURE 5.12
Latitude and
longitude are
attributes that
can usefully be
combined to
allow the
selection of an
area on a map
Source: *Keim*

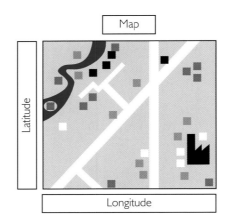

select a particular area of the map. There is no limit to the number (*N*) of attributes that can be handled, the number of histograms required being no more than *N*: recall that a scatterplot matrix increases in size as *N(N–1)/2*.

The fact that each house contributes to each histogram suggests an alternative presentation of histograms, as shown in Figure 5.13. Here, lines ('house-lines') join the contribution of each house to four attribute scales, leading to a presentation similar to Inselberg's parallel coordinate plots (Chapter 3). Animated enhancement of each line (that is, house) in turn can sometimes be helpful in gaining understanding of the displayed data (Tweedie *et al.*, 1994).

5.4.1 Sensitivity information

A major disadvantage of both the dynamic queries interface (Figure 5.1) and the illustrative example of a command-line query system is the absence of any direct guidance as to how a query might be modified to lead to more useful information. That guidance is especially required when a 'zero hit' or a 'too many hits' situation is encountered. Such a disadvantage can be markedly reduced by 'additive encoding' in which colour coding is applied, not only to those houses satisfying all attribute limits but, additionally and separately, to those failing one, two, three or more such limits. Thus, in the illustration of Figure 5.11, green indicates houses satisfying all limits, black those houses that fail one limit, dark gray those that fail two limits, and so on. It is now apparent how a limit may be usefully changed: a limit extended to include a black house will cause it to turn green. Even (Figure 5.14) for a query which identifies no acceptable (green) houses (that is, the 'zero hit' condition), the additional colour coding shows how limits can be relaxed to discover an acceptable house. Such information, shown by gray-scale encoding, is called sensitivity information, since it indicates the reduction in the number of violated limits achieved by the movement of a limit. The sensitivity information is an excellent example of the value of context: if only the green houses were displayed, no sensitivity information would be available and no guidance provided concerning possibly beneficial exploration.

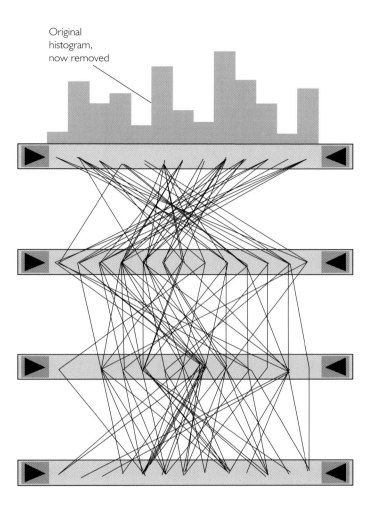

FIGURE 5.13
The principle of parallel coordinate plots can be combined with the Attribute Explorer

Original histogram, now removed

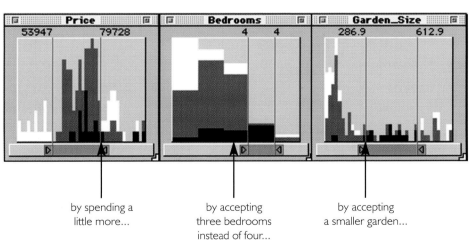

FIGURE 5.14
The 'zero hits' situation, but with black houses indicating possible limit relaxations

by spending a little more...

by accepting three bedrooms instead of four...

by accepting a smaller garden...

... an acceptable (green) house will appear

5.4.2 Summary information

It is not always easy, during exploration, to interpret a dynamic alteration of the color of the separate elements of a histogram. To aid such interpretation, summary information can be made available in the form of a yellow circle (Figure 5.15) positioned on the scale at the average of the attribute values of the selected group of objects. Now, when the range of *Price* is quickly moved up and down the corresponding scale, the yellow average circles on the *Bedrooms* and *Journey time* scales move correspondingly, allowing the relation between these attributes to be more readily discerned. Properties such as variance could similarly be encoded for easy understanding (Eick, 1994). In some circumstances, where display area is at a premium (see Chapter 9) the scale alone, without the associated histogram, might suffice.

FIGURE 5.15
The display of summary information, the yellow circle indicating the average of the values of the selected objects

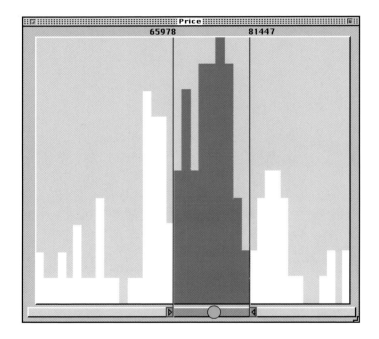

5.4.3 Dimensionality

A fundamental advantage of the concurrent display of histograms in the Attribute Explorer is that it provides a satisfactory solution to the problem of high dimensionality: the existence of more attributes simply requires the use of a proportionate number of histograms. This consistent use of a histogram places equal perceptual and presentational weight on each attribute, an essential property that would be virtually impossible to achieve by other means except for parallel coordinate plots.

5.4.4 Boolean operations

The facility illustrated in Figure 5.11 allowed the user to identify (in green) those houses which satisfied concurrent limits on *Price* AND *Bedrooms* AND *Garden size*. We emphasize the Boolean AND operation because, in fact, a wide variety of Boolean operations can be performed on the raw data. To render the Attribute Explorer more flexible for those who may wish to explore some other Boolean operations, the concept of the InfoCrystal (Spoerri, 1993) is relevant.

The basis of the InfoCrystal is simply illustrated for the case of three attributes A, B and C in Figure 5.16, which shows how the InfoCrystal is developed from the familiar Venn diagram. Thus, the 'topmost' diamond in the InfoCrystal identifies the operation 'A and (not B) and (not C)'. In the context of the Attribute Explorer, Tweedie (1997) has renamed the InfoCrystal as the Link Crystal to emphasize the fact that the Boolean operation links the limits on a number of histograms. The Link Crystal identifying the simple AND operation over all limits, and with sensitivity information additionally shown by the black and dark gray encoding of Figure 5.11, is shown in Figure 5.17. More complex queries can be constructed: the histograms and Link Crystal shown in Figure 5.18, for example, identify by yellow encoding those houses which fail the *price* limits but no others.

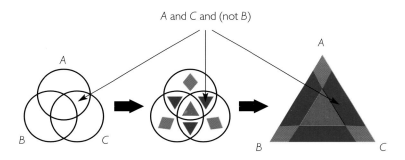

FIGURE 5.16
The development leading from a Venn diagram to the Link Crystal

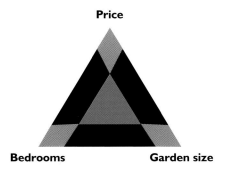

FIGURE 5.17
The Link Crystal corresponding to the Attribute Explorer display of Figure 5.11

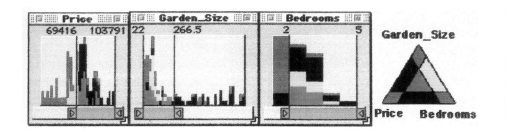

FIGURE 5.18
The Link Crystal and Attribute Explorer display for houses failing only the Price limit

5.4.5 *Fuzziness*

The reader may be tempted to point out that mathematical techniques exist which can handle the concept of fuzziness, that others are capable of optimization, and that these should play a major part in performing tasks such as the search for an acceptable house. Such techniques do exist, and have been developed to a fine art over decades, so it is useful to examine why they are not always ideal for the task of problem formulation and solution.

The underlying reason, stated at the start of this chapter, is that a user's problem is rarely formulated with precision, and that the first objective is to allow the user to gain knowledge of what is available. By contrast, an optimization program requires a user to specify in complete, precise and mathematical detail, what is being sought, as well as many other parameters such as the importance of getting the required number of bedrooms compared with that of keeping within a price limit. The program then returns a single solution *without explanation*; there is no indication, for example, of any trade-offs that were encountered. Overall, the user is left *uninformed*. If optimization techniques are to be employed, then very careful attention needs to be paid to the manner in which a user's knowledge and expertise can complement the power of the program: an example is provided by Colgan *et al*. (1995). With regard to fuzziness, the human brain is probably the best fuzzy computer around, especially when it is concurrently dealing with activities such as searching and exploring.

5.5 Very large databases

While there is no fundamental limit – except display area – to the number of objects that can be handled by the Attribute Explorer, it is useful to be aware of other visualization techniques that can also handle a large number of objects. One such technique is embodied in a visualization tool called VisDB (Keim *et al*., 1993), specifically designed to handle very large collections of data and to explore the limit in which a single pixel represents an object.

The principle underlying VisDB can be explained concisely by reference to an illustrative display (Figure 5.19). In the right-hand window are three vertical scales, each associated with an attribute. On each of these scales are two horizontal bars that can be positioned interactively by a user to indicate preferred lower and upper limits to the attribute's value. The number of objects thereby identified is indicated (1758 for Attribute 1) and the scale between the limits is coloured yellow. Since the satisfaction of *all* attribute limits by an object is of interest, and because many objects may fail to satisfy one or two limits, there is a facility for assigning a numerical 'weight' to each attribute to indicate the importance of satisfying the limits.

Together, the attribute limits and weights allow all objects to be placed in an order reflecting the extent to which each object satisfies the user's requirements. The question as to how the result can most usefully be displayed has been answered by ordering pixels (or sets of pixels) in a spiral pattern (Figure 5.20), with the 'best' objects at the center, and with colour coding to indicate the degree to which the objects satisfy requirements. Yellow denotes that all limits are satisfied, while other colours indicated on the left of the right-hand

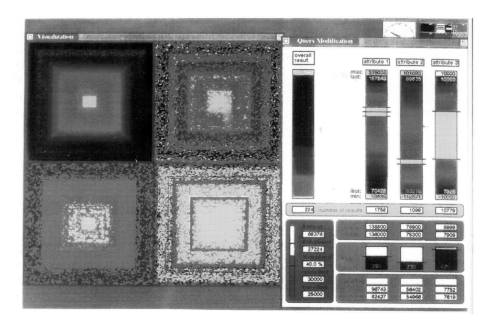

FIGURE 5.19
The VisDB
visualization
tool
Source: *Keim*

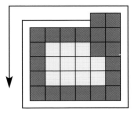

FIGURE 5.20
The spiral
arrangement of
pixels adopted
in the VisDB
visualization
tool

window show how the remainder are ordered in the spiral display. The result of forming these spiral displays is shown in the left-hand window in Figure 5.19. The top-left display is associated with the overall satisfaction of all limits according to the assigned weights, while the other three, based on the same ordering, show the extent to which the limits on each attribute are satisfied.

Such a display raises interesting questions as to desirable interaction mechanisms that can enhance the VisDB principle for particular applications. Nevertheless, it is important to note that, like the Attribute Explorer, VisDB offers no convenient mechanism for the display of images associated with attributes. Such a display (though for just a few objects), as well as other desirable features, is a characteristic of the Neighbourhood Explorer, to be discussed next.

5.6 The Neighbourhood Explorer

There are many circumstances in which only a relatively small set of data is involved. In house-hunting, for example, it would be quite unusual for a person to consider seriously houses in a very wide price range, such as £50,000 to £200,000. Usually, as a search approaches a conclusion, one is principally involved in the comparison of a relatively small number of houses, each of which is a relatively close neighbour – in the sense of attributes – of the others. In such a situation a simple rearrangement of the Attribute Explorer, as shown in Figure 5.21, positions houses relative to each other with regard to attributes such as *Price*, *number of Rooms* and *distance from vineyard*. Such attributes are associated with radial scales, with the currently examined house at the center: it also allows images to be associated with each house. Within a given sample set of houses it is the *ordering* of items which determines their relationships, rather than their attribute values, though a continuous linear scale might be adopted to emphasize, for example, relative prices. Exploration is achieved by dragging the image of a house which is of interest along its axis to the center, whereupon all of the axes are automatically realigned around this new origin.

FIGURE 5.21
Appearance of the Neighbourhood Explorer

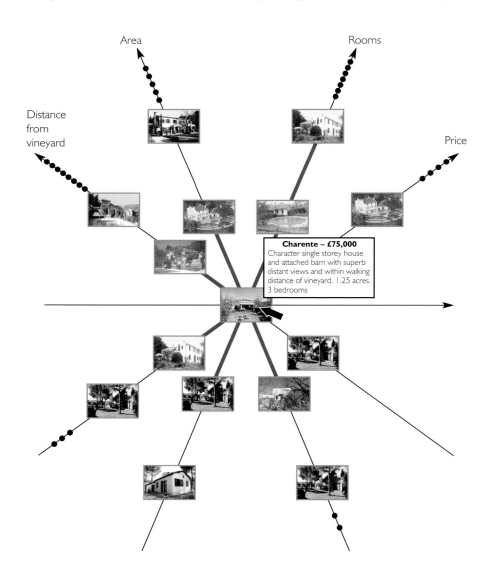

Area

Rooms

Distance from vineyard

Price

Charente – £75,000
Character single storey house and attached barn with superb distant views and within walking distance of vineyard. 1.25 acres. 3 bedrooms

It will be noticed from Figure 5.21, and especially from the house images, that a particular house is repeated on all scales. It is expected that such repetition will help the user to determine which house is 'closest' in some sense to the 'ideal'. To facilitate this process it is possible to include within the Explorer a virtual 'ideal house' to see how a currently examined house departs from that ideal (Figure 5.22). An added advantage is that the user is free to assign one dimension to the collection of examined houses in the sequence of their examination: that dimension is 'historical time' and again is not necessarily linear (Figure 5.23).

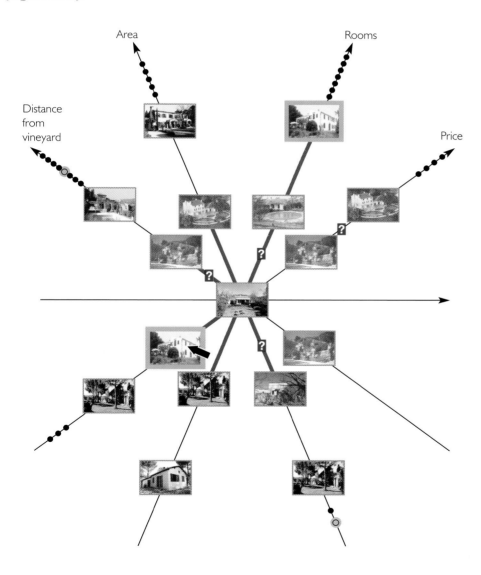

FIGURE 5.22
Incorporation of an ideal house in the Neighbourhood Explorer

FIGURE 5.23
Use of an axis
of the
Neighbourhood
Explorer to
record
potentially
interesting
houses

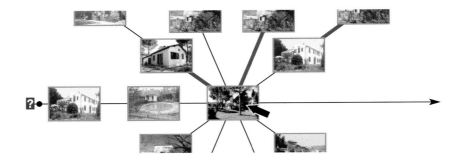

5.7 Musical visualization and composition

A memorable quotation from Bertrand Russell (1922) is that:

> *A good notation has a subtlety and suggestiveness that makes it seem, at times, like a live teacher.*

There are many fields which benefit from notation: mathematics, chemistry, choreography and others easily come to mind. So, of course, does musical notation. Conventional musical notation is reasonably familiar to most, but that familiarity has to be extremely intimate if it is to be used as a tool for composition. For most people, the sight or creation of a line of musical notation does not immediately lead to the visualization of how the corresponding tune will sound. To bring the power of composition closer to the lay person, experimental musical instruments have been devised whose output is not only aural – as one would expect – but also visual, and where changes made by direct manipulation within the externalization of the relevant data is either immediately or quickly heard.

The form of one such instrument is sketched in Figure 5.24; the metaphor on which it is based is the planetary system. In the center is the sun, and a collection of available planets is located at lower right. Each planet is associated with a given note, which appears as a label on the planet. If a planet is dragged within the circular area it comes under the 'gravitational influence' of the sun and, upon release, moves around it in an elliptical orbit. The user can also position an 'ear' somewhere in the planetary system. As a planet approaches and then recedes from the vicinity of the ear the 'sound' of that planet can be heard at a volume determined by how close the planet is to the ear. The effect of having a number of planets concurrently in orbit is reminiscent of a simple organ. Those with a knowledge of music can easily suggest collections of planets alternative to the pentatonic scale shown in Figure 5.24 and other effects such as chords or arpeggios. Though a simple interface, it proved in practice to be remarkably successful with users having no conventional musical skills, and the results of compositions by such people were pleasant to listen to. Basically, the success of the instrument is a result of its instantaneous response to manual changes in planet positions, and the simultaneity of the visual and aural presentation and hence the ease of exploration. An aural awareness of an unsuitable sound can immediately be correlated visually with the planet responsible, and the necessary corrective action to take quite easily deduced.

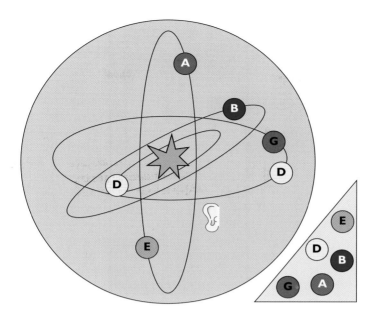

FIGURE 5.24
A musical instrument based on a 'planetary' metaphor

5.8 The Model Maker

An important task in engineering design is to find a mathematical relation (model) between the performances and parameters of an artefact, for the simple reason that the performance of that artefact for *any* chosen parameter values can then be predicted inexpensively before the costly process of manufacture. Suppose, for example, that someone has manufactured four samples of a gearbox, each with a different axle diameter, and has measured, for four different axle diameters (X), the torque (Y) that it can transmit before damage occurs (Figure 5.25(a)). A simple mathematical relation somehow 'fitted' to the data (Figure 5.25(b)) can then be used (Figure 5.25(c)) with some confidence to calculate the effect of other diameters, and obviate the need for additional – and usually expensive – measurements. While the value of such a model is clear, its derivation can be difficult. It is here that information visualization can help.

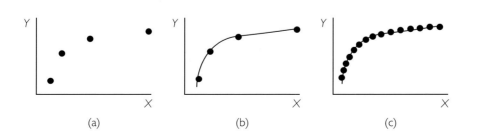

(a)   (b)   (c)

FIGURE 5.25
The derivation and use of a mathematical model

Typically, the type of relation fitted to available data is a polynomial of the form:

$$\text{Performance } (P) = a + bx_1 + cx_2 + dx_1x_2 + ex_1^2 + fx_2^2 + \ldots \qquad (5.1)$$

where, in this illustrative example, there are two parameters (x_1 and x_2) and one performance (P) of interest.[4] The fitting task is then the selection of appropriate values of the coefficients a, b, c and so on. There are two components of the fitting task. One is to choose which terms (for example, dx_1x_2) to include in the model. The next is to find the appropriate numerical values of their coefficients (for example, d for the term dx_1x_2).

The person carrying out the 'fitting' has two conflicting requirements. They want to keep the relation as simple as possible, but they also want the relation to be sufficiently accurate. The solution is to present them with a display which allows them to choose whether or not to include a particular term in the polynomial, but which additionally offers support by showing the estimated accuracy of the resulting model. The freedom to choose which term to next include in the model results in there being a large number of possibilities, so an essential property of any supportive visualization tool is to display the currently proposed model in the context of all possible models 'one step away'.

An interface called the Model Maker (Tweedie *et al.*, 1998) is shown in Figure 5.26. Each square represents a single term in the polynomial being fitted to measured data, and has one of the three possible appearances shown in Figure 5.27. A black inscribed circle denotes a term already included in the model, whereas white circles are associated with terms that are not yet included. The size of those circles provides a measure of how useful the term is (black) or how useful it can be if included in the model (white). A white background indicates that the term can be added or removed on its own, whereas a gray background indicates that, for heuristic mathematical reasons, the term's inclusion requires other terms to be included at the same time. The modeler

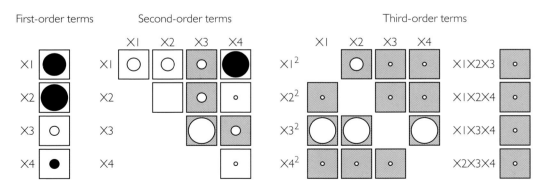

FIGURE 5.26
The interface to the Model Maker

---

[4] The need to consider four or many more performances and a similar number of parameters would not be regarded as unusual in engineering design.

A **black** circle indicates a term already **included** in the model

The term is **moderately** valuable (**medium** size circle)

The term is statistically **legal** (**white** background)

A **white** circle indicates a term **not** yet included in the model

Circle size indicates that it would be **very** valuable (**large** circle)

The term is statistically **legal** (**white** background)

A **white** circle indicates a term **not** yet included in the model

Circle size indicates that it would be **moderately** valuable (**medium** circle)

The term cannot be included on its own (**gray** background)

FIGURE 5.27 Representation of the three possible states of a term in a mathematical model

might start by looking at the single ('first-order') terms, such as bx_1 and cx_2, each represented by a square, and by searching for the largest interior circle: this is, by definition (Figure 5.27), the one whose inclusion is likely to be most beneficial to a good 'fit'. Its inclusion in the model (with a coefficient calculated by a background algorithm) is achieved by a single mouse-click on the selected square, whereupon the circle will turn black to confirm its inclusion. Concurrently, a value of a 'goodness of fit' of the current model is updated. The modeler then continues the process, including more terms and possibly higher order ones, until a satisfactory balance is achieved between goodness of fit and the model's simplicity. The basic fitting actions just described are complemented by many other facilities in the actual Model Maker. An example of a fitted polynomial is provided as Equation 9.1 in Chapter 9.

The principal motivation for the development of the Model Maker is the generally low level of statistical knowledge possessed by design engineers, coupled with the typical absence of domain knowledge possessed by statisticians. The interface described is a visualization tool like all others described in this chapter in that it allows dynamic exploration among a large number of possible outcomes, but differs in the sense that considerable computation proceeds in the background to compute the sensitivity information (the sizes of the interior circles), the corresponding coefficients (that is, a, b, c, d, etc.) and the goodness of fit.

CHAPTER 6

Internal Models, their Formation and Interpretation

6.1 The need for internal models

In Chapter 1 we adopted the definition that information visualization is the formation of an internal (mental) model of some data, and suggested that the model is created through sight of some display of that data. The very good reason for seeking an internal model is to have a better understanding of the artefact, scheme or situation to which the data refers, and to be able to interpret that model (Figure 6.1) in some useful way, perhaps to make a decision. Simple examples of such models, the sort of interpretation that may follow and the location in this book where the example is discussed, include:

■ The engineering designer who observes the value of some property X of an artefact as the value of some other property Y is manually or automatically

FIGURE 6.1
The interpretation of an internal model

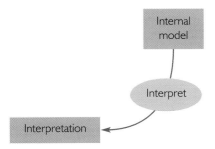

varied, and forms an internal model of the relation between X and Y. The interpretation may be that there appears to be some trade-off between the two properties (Chapter 9).

- A house-buyer who discovers that a readiness to pay more does not make more houses available. The interpretation may be that the discovery of an affordable house needs the relaxation of one or more other limits (Chapter 5).

- Certain crops respond well to a particular treatment so further study to investigate the cost of treatments is desirable (Chapter 2).

- As well as the route I usually take, there is also a Circle Line Underground route direct from South Kensington to Liverpool Street station. The model lacks a comparison of journey times.

Since internal models appear to be so closely associated with information visualization we examine, in this chapter, the nature of those models, their interpretation and how they are formed. In doing so we move some way towards identifying implicit guidelines to support the designer of visualization tools.

Before going into detail it should be remarked that even though billions of words have been written about mental processes, there is even now a lack of consensus among professionals regarding the concepts involved. Gibson (1997), for example, in his book *Theories of Visual Perception* remarks that a more appropriate title might be '*Some* theories of visual perception'. It is nevertheless useful, in the limited space of this chapter, to introduce some generally accepted concepts related to internal models and which, together with some illustrative examples, will hopefully provide some basis for productive thought about the design of effective visualization tools.

6.2 Navigation

Our discussion will be based on a framework (Figure 6.2) for the human activity we call navigation, one component of which is the user's internal model which is of such importance to information visualization. We begin by briefly explaining the framework in outline (Spence, 1999) and then examining each component

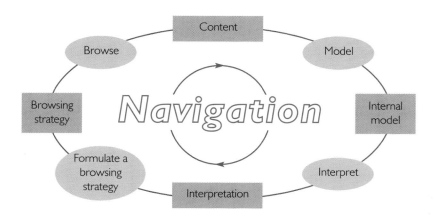

FIGURE 6.2
A framework for navigation

in detail, in all cases using illustrative examples drawn from earlier chapters. The framework will be seen to describe the process of navigation of information space where, initially we broadly define navigation as the creation and interpretation of an internal mental model.

The activity[1] identified in Figure 6.2 as browsing occurs, for example, when a user scans a display to 'see what's there'. They may be looking at a Spotfire display of pollutants (Chapter 5) in order to see what pattern emerges. The modeling of that pattern results in the internal model (or 'cognitive map'): in the same example it could be the association of pollution with some geographic feature. Interpretation of that model follows; perhaps the likelihood that other pollutants may have the same source. Next, based on that interpretation, the user can formulate a new browsing strategy; that could be a decision to display two particular pollutants together to see, again by browsing, if some correlation exists. The entire framework is that of navigation in the sense that the internal model is being created and explored. The overall intention or goal which requires navigation to occur may be a general desire to gain insight into (that is, to visualize) the origin of pollution within Sweden.

Since the framework of Figure 6.2 currently refers only to internal (mental) processes we shall gradually extend it to include essential external features such as the externalization of the data that the user is browsing. First, however, we examine some properties of internal models.

6.3 Internal models

6.3.1 *Cognitive maps*

We often refer to an internal model as a cognitive map. Tversky (1993) points out that 'as mental constructs available to mental inspection, cognitive maps are presumed to be like real maps available to real inspection'. For example, having worked in London for many years I possess a reasonable if limited internal model of the London Underground railway system. For short journeys from Imperial College (close to South Kensington station) I need not look at a printed map, and only miss my destination if reading a particularly gripping book. But for less familiar journeys I need, in order to enhance my confidence, to glance at the printed map (the so-called externalization of the relevant data) before starting my journey. In so doing I'm initially and briefly referring to my internal model to identify the parts that need clarifying but then, by looking at the map, I can extend my internal model sufficiently to be able to undertake the journey. I might also choose, in fact, to create a new but related model which is simpler to remember – at least temporarily – for the particular journey: it might be of the form 'east on the Piccadilly, then east on the red line'. Although much remains to be discovered about memory (Solso, 1998), sufficient is already known with some degree of confidence for a simple account relevant to information visualization to be presented here (Norman, 1983; Waugh and Norman, 1965).

---

[1] In Figure 6.2 and throughout the chapter, activities are coded blue, their results (which can form the argument of another activity) are coded light purple, while the externalizations (that is, displays) of data are coded yellow.

6.3.2 Cognitive collage

In many situations it is more realistic to speak of a collection of cognitive maps or, as Tversky (1993) calls it, a cognitive collage. Thus, as a result of my journeys on the London Underground, I can recall in detail a number of separate segments, but have difficulty 'joining them up'. Not surprisingly, the existence of a collage can lead to misinterpretations. A familiar illustration of errors that can emerge when accessing two items within a collage relates to the following question:

'Which city is farther west, Reno or Los Angeles?'

A common answer is 'Los Angeles', because that city is associated with California and Reno is associated with Nevada, which is east of California. However, reference to a real map shows (Figure 6.3) that Reno is *west* of Los Angeles. Association of Reno with Nevada and Los Angeles with California can be thought of as one item in memory, and the relative locations of Nevada and California as another, and the danger lies in the simple combination of these two items.

FIGURE 6.3
A map showing the states of California and Nevada, and the cities of Los Angeles and Reno

6.3.3 Incompleteness of a mental model

The fact that an internal model is not a single homogeneous entity has already been stressed by reference to the concept of a cognitive collage. In addition, the possibility of it being incomplete must also be appreciated. For example, our internal model of the shape of different countries is of little help in recognition if the representation of that country is tilted through an angle, if the relative size of the country is not shown, and if context is removed: try identifying the countries whose shapes appear in Figure 6.4! The problem here is that each country has been seen on so many occasions in an 'upright' position and in proximity to other familiar countries.[2]

---

[2] The countries of Figure 6.4 are, from left to right, British Isles, France, Italy, India and Africa.

FIGURE 6.4
The relative size and orientation of some countries have been altered – identify them!

6.3.4 Resistance to change

In the event that I *have* to consult the London Underground map to enhance my mental model of the part I plan to traverse I would expect to see, pasted to a wall of some station, the familiar map (Figure 6.5). However if, overnight (Figure 6.6), someone had removed all the Underground maps and replaced them with new maps printed upside-down, but with the lettering upside-up, then my browsing and interpretation of the (perfectly valid) map would be far more difficult, simply because of the challenge of simultaneously understanding two maps, one internal and the other external. I would also worry that the 'old map' would never be printed again, thereby requiring me to begin construction of a new internal model and, simultaneously, suppression of the old one. This situation may appear farcical, but the electronic equivalent often occurs on a computer screen where externalizations are so easy to modify.

FIGURE 6.5
The London Underground map

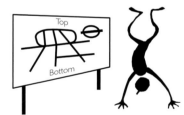

FIGURE 6.6
An inverted London Underground map

6.3.5 Inertial effects

Sometimes an externalization of a given set of data has to change in order for some insight to be gained. An example (Robertson *et al.*, 1991) is provided by the so-called Cone-Tree representation of hierarchical data, to be discussed in more detail in Chapter 8. At one instant of time the tree may appear as shown in Figure 6.7, perhaps to allow a user to observe the relation between three people (including close colleagues) in an organization. A later need to bring different data to the fore would require rotation of one or more cones (Figure 6.8). If the change is abrupt (in other words, if Figure 6.7 is *immediately* replaced by Figure 6.8) then, although the newly required data may easily be visible, one's internal model of the rest of the cone tree may well be destroyed or, at best, not rehearsed.

  To overcome this potential disadvantage, the inventors of the Cone-Tree arranged for the transition to proceed smoothly over a period of about one

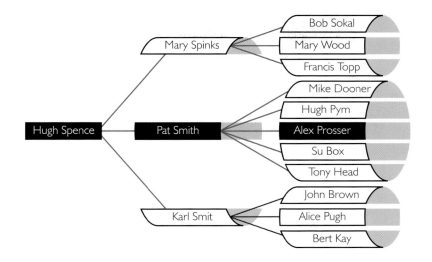

FIGURE 6.7
A Cone-Tree representation of hierarchical data: a company organization chart

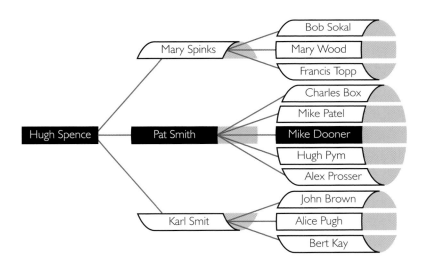

FIGURE 6.8
A new presentation of the Cone-Tree of Figure 6.7, corresponding to a new focus

second. In this way the cone rotations are sufficiently slow that the user does not lose awareness of the spatial form of the model and have to construct a new one: the user is being shown how the two states relate to each other. In the video presentation of the Cone-Tree concept it is pointed out that ' . . . the perceptual phenomenon of object constancy enables the user to track substructure relations without thinking about it'. As we shall see in Chapter 8, the user is additionally helped by sight of the 'shadow' cast by the cones on a base plane which, in the illustrations of Figures 6.7 and 6.8, would be vertical and to the right of the tree.

6.3.6 Model robustness

When we say we are familiar with something we are in effect saying that we have a well-established and robust internal model of that thing. Such a property can be exploited. One example occurred in Chapter 4 where magnification was the encoding mechanism: one's approximate feeling for the size of various countries and their relative spatial layout is such that magnification can provide a reasonable qualitative indication of some property associated with each country.

6.4 Model formation

We have already seen, in earlier chapters, the many circumstances in which an internal model can be formed, and the various activities that can assist that formation; the selection of a new price limit is an example (Chapter 5). It is worth subjecting these activities to a more detailed study in order to draw more generic conclusions.

At the most primitive level in information visualization, the user typically views a collection of items on a display screen. As the user's eye moves over the display, those items in foveal vision (Anstis, 1967; Bouma, 1970) are registered with more precision than those in peripheral vision: there is a visual acuity gradient moving out from the fovea. We shall refer to this activity as browsing, defined as the registration (or elicitation or assessment) of content. As an example, the tourist visiting an unfamiliar town and consulting a newly acquired map may almost immediately notice a green area, a blue area, an area of narrow winding streets, a factory area and a railway line, *though initially without forming an internal model*. Similarly the diner visiting a new restaurant will scan the menu to see what dishes are available and how the menu is laid out. The term 'scan-browse' has been used by Carmel *et al.* (1992) to describe this activity.

The content acquired by browsing is, probably almost immediately, integrated (Figure 6.9) in some way to begin forming a mental map, a process referred to as 'review-browse' by Carmel *et al.* (1992) and as *modeling* in this book. Thus, the tourist will note that the narrow streets are close to the harbor, and that the railway line passes close to their hotel. Similarly the diner will have quickly formed an impression of the standard of cuisine, the range of choice, the general price range and the likelihood of finding something attractive to their palate.

FIGURE 6.9
Browsing of externalized data leads to an internal model

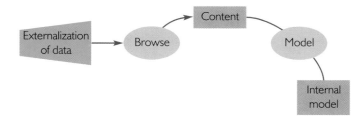

6.4.1 *Externalization*

The interaction designer must, of course, arrange for relevant data to be externalized so that it can be browsed (Figure 6.9). While such externalization is normally in graphic form on a computer display, it can also be visual, aural, tactile or olfactory. In the physical world it could be all four, for example, during a medical examination when the physician views a diseased limb, manipulates it, listens to it and is sensitive to any odour, all in order to form an internal model of the underlying problem. For the moment we concentrate on the more common graphic externalization while acknowledging that other sensory mechanisms might be able to provide additional or alternative beneficial capacity.

6.4.2 Perception and cognition

A familiar model provided by cognitive scientists, and relevant to the process of browsing leading to the formation of an internal model is shown in Figure 6.10. The process termed 'perception' ends with a representation in memory, but as yet no meaning. The representation is then subjected to the process of cognition (Humphreys and Bruce, 1989) in which a model representing some understanding is established in memory. The processes of perception and cognition are, in fact, extremely complex and not fully understood. We shall therefore work with the navigation framework of Figure 6.2 and use the verb 'model' to describe that part of the cognition process that takes the result of browsing and forms it into an internal model or an addition to an existing model. We already have, of course, many internal models, and some of these may be relevant to the task currently being undertaken, so that what is labeled 'model' in Figure 6.9 should be placed in the context of other internal models (Figure 6.11) and a return arrow added to indicate that the formation of an internal model may well require reference to an already existing one.

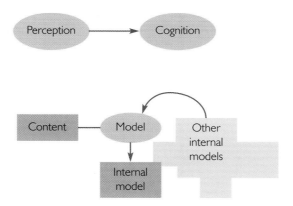

FIGURE 6.10
The processes of perception and cognition

FIGURE 6.11
A model relevant to a particular task may be formed by reference to an existing model and may then form part of it

6.4.3 Weighted browsing

For the purpose of describing the browsing and modeling process in a way that might help our understanding of information visualization, we introduce the concept of weighted browsing. In a typical browsing situation a user – for example the tourist or diner referred to above – will not assess all the content, partly because there is so much of it and partly because much might be suspected to be of little or no interest. Thus, when handed the menu in an unfamiliar Italian restaurant I initially put low weighting on (in other words, I have little interest in) the soups and pizzas, I put average weighting on pasta dishes and a very high weighting on scallopini marsala and chocolate profiteroles. The internal model I first create by such 'selective attention' will thereby contain little or no information about pizzas, while the presence of scallopini and profiteroles will certainly be highlighted.

6.4.4 *Externalization for browsing*

For a user to browse and gradually build an internal model there must obviously be something there to browse! The question therefore arises as to how data should be presented on the display screen to ensure effective browsing (Figure 6.12). We begin with two contrasting illustrations regarding externalization design.

FIGURE 6.12
Externalization of the data that is to be browsed

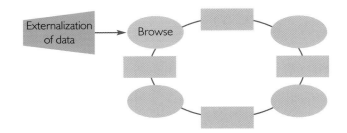

The display of Figure 6.13, making sparse use of display space, offers an encyclopaedia user a choice of Art, Science or Religion, the selection of one of these options taking the user to the corresponding subordinate menu. These three options can certainly be browsed, but only allow a very simple model to be created. In fact, their main purpose may legitimately have been to allow the user to reach a particular target word as conveniently and quickly as possible (Norman, 1991) and with no intention that the user should build an internal model, of something as large as an encyclopaedia, to facilitate later use.

FIGURE 6.13
A menu system which does not support extensive browsing, possibly intentionally so

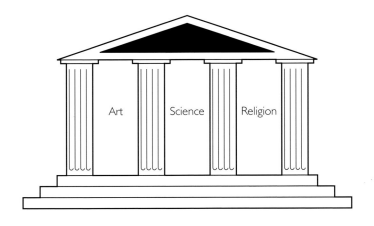

By contrast, the opening scene (Figure 6.14) of the CDi title *Richard Scarry's Busiest Neighborhood Disc Ever* makes full use of the available screen space. Moreover, in the opening scene, what is displayed changes automatically and smoothly, in a 'panning' mode. As a result, after a period of about ten seconds, the user has been able, without performing any control action at all, to browse an area about five times the size of the screen. As a consequence, that user has been enabled to build a reasonable internal model of the content sufficient to decide what next to explore in some detail.

FIGURE 6.14
A presentation offering considerable opportunity for browsing and the formation of an internal model

Source: *Reproduced by permission of Philips Media*

6.4.5 Influence as content

The definition of browsing is not limited to the viewing of a fixed and passively displayed object. A particularly valuable form of browsing, encountered in the dynamic queries examples in Chapter 5, takes the form of registering cause and effect – a sort of 'ping-pong' browsing often associated with exploration stimulated by a 'what if?' question (Figure 6.15). Thus, in the house-seeking example, movement of an upper price limit ('ping'), together with the resulting effect ('pong') constitutes a sample of some relation, and therefore is a form of content which is browsed and may then be incorporated into the internal model.

FIGURE 6.15
'Ping-pong'
browsing

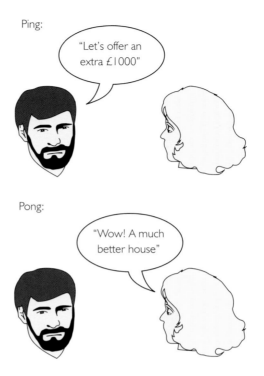

6.4.6 Short-term memory

One feature of the human cognitive system that constrains activities such as modeling is short-term memory (STM). Although controversy still surrounds this concept it is known that STM has a very limited storage and processing capacity, but the possibility of a trade-off between the two. That STM is not only severely limited, but requires *rehearsal* to maintain its content, was demonstrated in a classic experiment by Peterson and Peterson (1959). In their experiment subjects were read a three-letter cluster and asked to recall it after varying periods of time during which subjects had to count backwards by threes from a three-digit number presented immediately after the three-letter cluster:

> *Experimenter:* CHJ 506
> *Subject:* 506, 503, 500, 497 . . . (until time to repeat the three-letter cluster).

The experimental results, shown in Figure 6.16, show that recall is seriously eroded in the absence of rehearsal.

6.4.7 The magic number seven plus or minus two

How extensive is STM? Short term memory is generally accepted to be able to hold around seven 'units of information', hence the title of George Miller's (1956) paper, 'The magical number seven, plus or minus two: Some limits on our capacity for processing information'. Thus, if asked to remember and then

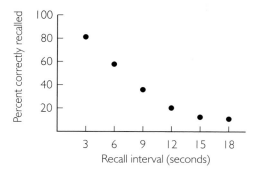

FIGURE 6.16
Recall as a
function of
recall interval,
when rehearsal
was prevented

recall a string of letters, it would be difficult to do so without significant error if more than seven letters were involved. However, if the letters happened to be the following sequence:

I B M B B C C I A F B I S O S

then it is likely that more than seven letters would be recalled, but only because the subject would have been able to 'chunk' each group of three in view of their familiarity. Indeed, it is widely accepted that a subject would only be able to remember around seven 'chunks' of information.

How is STM relevant to information visualization? The basis for an illustration has already been provided in Chapter 5 by both the Dynamic Queries tool and the Attribute Explorer. As the use of either of these tools proceeds, new images containing potentially useful information are examined and, at the same time, new questions formulated. Thus, in the course of searching for a house to buy, not all presentations will have been remembered.[3] Since some intermediate results may later be thought to have been significant ('maybe we *could* go for that larger house – remember? – and take in paying guests'), but might be difficult to recall in detail, it could be useful to provide some means – such as a simple 'tagging' mechanism – whereby potentially interesting intermediate situations could be recorded for later retrieval and re-examination.

The activity of electronic circuit design provides another example. In Chapter 2 it was shown how data concerning the effect, on the performance of an electronic circuit, of small changes in individual component values could be encoded by the size of circles superimposed on the corresponding component symbols (Figure 6.17). Moreover, animation was employed to show the manner in which these circles vary in size as the frequency varies over the range from bass to treble and back again. What we know about STM suggests that, if there were three important and broadly distinguishable regions of frequency (for example, bass, mid and treble) it might just be possible to observe and recall the nature of size changes for two or three components.

---

[3] Of possibly equal importance, neither will the questions which ultimately led to the formation of these presentations.

FIGURE 6.17
With the animated circles it may be possible to recall, in outline, the size changes occurring at bass, mid and treble frequencies for around three components

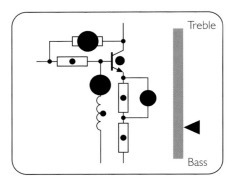

6.5 Model interpretation

The execution of any task involving information visualization will be motivated by the user's intention and influenced by many factors. One of these is the user's internal model. Another is the visible externalization of some data. A decision as to how – as well as whether – to proceed will depend upon an interpretation of these sources of information (Figure 6.18). Once an interpretation is available a decision can be made as to how and whether further browsing should proceed, or whether the original overall intention should be modified. We begin with an example from Chapter 5.

FIGURE 6.18
Interpretation of the internal model and externalized data

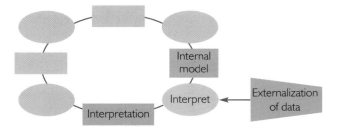

The house-seeker may well have visited a number of houses and have built an internal model of certain features: the presence of nice looking schools near Pearson's Park, the worrying occurrence of graffiti near the otherwise attractive lakeside cottages and the steep rise in house prices as one moves towards the centre of Thurstonbury. The house-seeker may well have jotted down some of these observations as a memory aid. They may also be viewing an externalization of some data – a map, perhaps, or a histogram, or some images of houses that have been tagged as being affordable and potentially satisfactory. On the basis of all this information, partly internal and partly external, the user's interpretation may be that no further exploration is necessary, since internal and external models are sufficiently detailed that a visit to an estate agent is now appropriate to obtain more detailed information regarding the candidate houses. On the other hand an interpretation may indicate the likelihood of real bargains along the Scottswood Road, in which case an appropriate display to permit browsing in that area must be obtained. In that sense the term 'browsing' includes 'locomotion' to a new area. That locomotion may be physical (as in a car) or virtual, the latter possibly involving only an eye movement.

6.5.1 Interpretation of externalized data

We begin by selecting three illustrations of how externalized data can be interpreted. The first (Figure 6.19) is a particular presentation ('bifocal' or 'fisheye' – see Chapter 7) of data in which parts are 'bent backwards' so as to allow everything to fit into the display area.

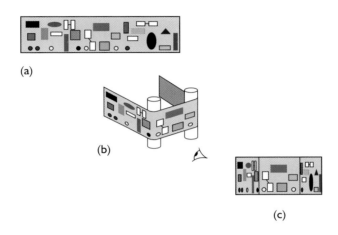

(a)

(b)

(c)

FIGURE 6.19
Principle of the bifocal display
(a) Information space, much larger than the display
(b) The same space 'wrapped around' two uprights and viewed as shown
(c) The view seen by a user, and scrollable as suggested in (b)

Since items in the peripheral areas would be unreadable because they are 'squashed', the text and similar detail is automatically removed;[4] nevertheless, the colour of each item is discernable. Thus, a red rectangle towards the left edge of the information space denotes a letter from my boss, an item that can be scrolled into the central region to expand horizontally and become readable. Here my interpretation is that there is an urgent letter presently located in iconic form towards the left of the display. Thus, an important property of the display is that it provides a measure of *sensitivity*: I can easily form some idea as to the extent to which I must scroll the information space to achieve my goal of reading the letter from my boss.

A second example is provided by the black houses in Figure 5.14: they provide some measure of the direction as well as the distance one has to move a particular limit in order to acquire the corresponding data. They provide a measure of sensitivity, or a 'gradient' with respect to houses that fail only one limit. A similar measure of sensitivity is provided by the tight coupling concept (Ahlberg, 1996) illustrated in Figure 5.6.

A third example, involving the aural presentation of information, was provided by the Media Room (Bolt, 1979). Here (Figure 6.20), a user panning across an image of the MIT campus on a screen measuring 11 feet by 8 feet becomes

---

[4] See the discussion of semantic zooming in Chapter 7, Section 7.8.1.

FIGURE 6.20
The Media
Room at MIT

Source: *MIT*

aware, on hearing the (stereo) roar of a football crowd, that there is a large and well-packed football stadium 'somewhere off the left edge of the screen'. Again the act of interpretation could be classified as one of 'gradient perception' or an awareness of sensitivity.

Although the concepts of 'gradient perception' and sensitivity can be useful, and may even be widely applicable, they will in many cases be an oversimplification of the manner in which data is interpreted. The topic is complicated by the fact that interpretations may be formed consciously or unconsciously; may be based on part or the whole of the externalized and internalized data; and may well be influenced by existing domain knowledge possessed by the user. Also, as we shall see in the next section, the interpretation could well be influenced by knowledge of the available browsing mechanisms that can be harnessed to exploit the interpretation.

6.5.2 Model adequacy

One aspect of interpretation that must always be borne in mind is the *adequacy* of a model. This property is perhaps best illustrated by analogy with the process of fitting a mathematical model to some available quantitative data. For example, if the data about how some property X varies as some parameter Y is changed is contained within five data points (Figure 6.21), it could be dangerous to base any interpretation on a smooth curve (Figure 6.22) fitted to the data, since the *actual* variation of X with Y might be as shown in Figure 6.23. It is in situations like this that domain knowledge and experience can play an important part and, if appro-

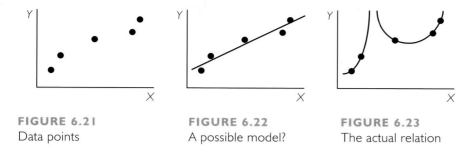

FIGURE 6.21
Data points

FIGURE 6.22
A possible model?

FIGURE 6.23
The actual relation

priate, help identify the fact that a model is impoverished in some respect. If a model is impoverished in any way it may be difficult or impossible to perceive any valid gradient or sensitivity indication or make any useful interpretation. Such a situation might obtain, for example, after examining only four or five houses in the house-seeking scenario of Chapter 5, so that questions such as 'can we increase the number of bedrooms without increasing the price?' simply cannot be answered with any useful degree of confidence. In this case the interpretation would be to the effect that further content should be browsed.

6.6 The formulation of browsing strategy

Until now we have said little about browsing strategies and how they are formulated. It is unfortunate that definitions of browsing offered in the literature sometimes imply a rather unstructured and random activity, perhaps with serendipitous intent, and even with a hint that it might not have been consciously planned. That is one possible browsing strategy, but only one among many. When I pick up my copy of *The Times* newspaper I *know* where the weather report is, on which page the obituaries are to be found, where the 'Comment' is and where, on a Saturday, the humorous 'Letters to the Editor' are positioned, and I habitually register their content in that order. My planned but unconscious browsing is brisk, is essentially asking 'what's there?' and is followed by a decision about what I want first to read in detail.

Nevertheless, though my browsing is planned, that plan may suddenly be abandoned, and my activity become opportunistic, upon noticing the obituary of my old teacher. But other, entirely different strategies are possible, perhaps using a different source of data; one might, for example, read the 'Summary' provided on the back page of *The Times* instead. The question is, how is my strategy, both global and detailed, determined, and how can the externalization of data best be organized to help decide upon the browsing action (Figure 6.24)? And for interactive (as opposed to passive) displays, how can the interaction best be designed to support the formulation of a browsing strategy?

6.6.1 Cognitive determinant

There are two determinants of the formulation of browsing strategy (Tweedie, 1995). One is cognitive, based either upon the interpretation I have made or as a result of a new idea (Figure 6.25), but not directly influenced by what is

FIGURE 6.24
The formulation
of a browsing
strategy, partly
influenced by
the
externalization
of data

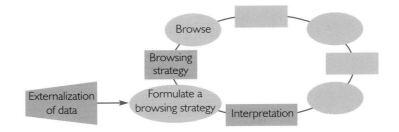

displayed. The interpretation may be to the effect that navigation should be terminated because, for example, a small group of houses worthy of more detailed consideration has been identified. Alternatively it may be to the effect that the original intention is not yet satisfied and that a particular exploration – say, the variation of an upper limit on *price* – is now needed. Such a conscious and cognitively planned browsing strategy could then be formulated. I may, on the other hand, suddenly decide to adopt a new course of action to see if it proves helpful, that of checking an estate agent's brochure: a cognitively initiated opportunistic strategy.

FIGURE 6.25
Cognitive and
perceptual
determinants of
planned and
opportunistic
strategies

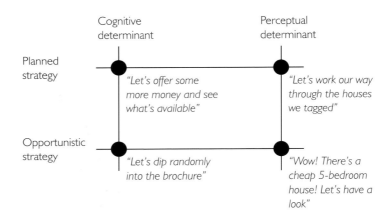

6.6.2 *Perceptual determinant*

The other determinant is perceptual. In other words, the strategy I formulate is influenced directly by what I see displayed on the screen. Consider, for example, the screen display of Figure 6.26, one not very different from the Attribute Explorer encountered in Chapter 5. The key to various user actions that are now possible lies in the controls, associated with various affordances, that are provided in the display, and which can be used to rearrange that display as discussed in Chapter 2. These controls are briefly described by annotations outside the screen area in Figure 6.26.

Other features of the display which can influence my actions include, for example, the black houses, the general distributions of the histograms and the 'ineffective range of limit' (Figure 5.6) indicators. Yet another feature of the display is associated with houses thought to be sufficiently interesting at the time they were first encountered to be recorded for later reconsideration. Sight of those cir-

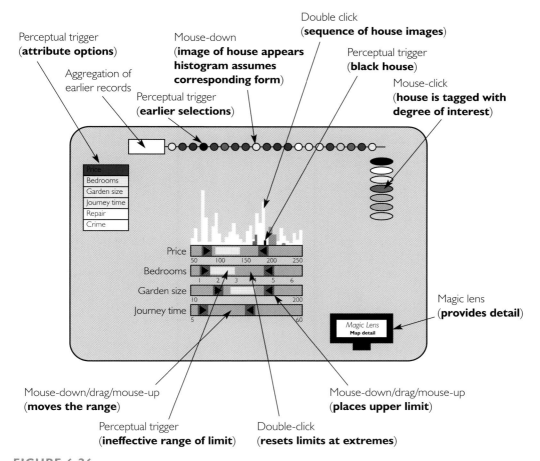

FIGURE 6.26

An application of the Attribute Explorer, illustrating a rich collection of controls and perceptual triggers as well as data

cles might prompt me to decide that my next browsing strategy will be to re-examine one of those records: a planned action stimulated perceptually. Similarly I may notice that other tools are available that I have not used before: an example is the Magic Lens (described later in Chapter 7) which, like a magnifying glass, can be moved over a component of the histogram to reveal aspects of the underlying data that do not appear within the Attribute Explorer, aspects such as the appearance of an individual house or a map containing locations of interest. On the other hand, sight of the display may lead to a perceptually initiated opportunistic action – also called a situated action (Suchman, 1987) – such as a shift of focus to an area near the factory where a very cheap but large house has been noticed. As pointed out before, the new browsing strategy can include a shift of location.

Whether prompted cognitively or perceptually, the execution of the selected browsing strategy may lead either to the enhancement of a currently considered internal model or the initiation of another internal model, part of a collage (Tversky, 1993).

6.7 Comment

Based on the above discussion, navigation might more fully be defined as cognitively directed movement in information (or physical) space based on the interpretation of a mental model and/or externalized data. Although one aim of the navigation framework is to provide a basis for organized thought about information visualization it does not provide precise rules for the designer of a visualization tool to follow. The design of such a tool – like the design of any worthwhile artefact – is an exceedingly complex (and little understood) process. Nevertheless the framework can provide a useful reference during the course of visualization tool design, and is frequently referred to in later chapters.

CHAPTER 7

Presentation

7.1 A problem

Many of us have found ourselves with a report that has to be completed by a deadline, with the result (Figure 7.1) that the dining room table, extended to its twelve-guest state, is covered by piles of paper as well as reports, books, clippings and slides; perhaps with more arranged on the floor and on a couple of chairs. There may even be piles on top of piles. Such a presentation of vital information makes a lot of sense: everything relevant is to hand (we hope!) and, moreover, its very visibility acts as a reminder (Bolt, 1984) of what might be relevant at any particular juncture, possibly triggering a situated action (Suchman, 1987). In this environment I can concentrate on creative tasks rather than organization.

Despite the availability of high-resolution displays and powerful workstations I still write most of my reports in this way. Why? Because the display area provided by the typical workstation is far too small to support, visibly, all the sources that are relevant to my composition.

7.2 The presentation problem

I am not alone in the sense of having too much data to fit onto a small screen. A very large and expensive screen, for example, would be needed to display the London Underground map in sufficient detail (Figure 1.1), and it would be difficult or impossible to present, on a normal display, the complete organization

FIGURE 7.1
Support for
report
preparation!

chart of IBM or ICI. Moreover, the recent emergence of small and mobile information and communication devices such as PDAs and wearable displays has
additionally identified a pressing need for a solution to the 'too much data, too
little display area' problem: the *presentation problem*. How can it be solved,
mindful of the need to support the activity of visualizing the underlying data?

7.2.1 Scrolling

An obvious solution is to scroll the data into and out of the visible area. In other
words, to provide a means whereby a long document can be moved past a
window until it reaches the required 'page' (Figure 7.2). This mechanism is
widely used, but carries with it many penalties. One relates to the 'Where am I?'
problem: I'm working on Chapter 2, (it may be Section 2.3, I'm not sure) and I
want to remind myself of a figure that is in Chapter 5, it may be in Section 5.3 –
or was it 5.6? All I can do is operate the scrolling mechanism and look out for the
figure I need, albeit assisted by various cues such as the page number indicated
in the scrolling mechanism. With a scrolling mechanism, most of a document is
hidden from view. I have the same problem when using a microfilm reader. A
similar difficulty applies to my use of the famous London 'A to Z' street directory.
I'm driving along a road that goes off the edge of the page, so I desperately need
whatever page contains the continuation of that road (and quickly!). Even if I get
it, I will typically have trouble locating the same road on the new page. These and
other similar problems can be ameliorated by the provision of *context*. Much of
this chapter, in fact, is concerned with *deciding how to provide context*.

7.2.2 Context map

Some drawbacks of the scrolling technique can be ameliorated by the provision
of a map with the location of the detail of interest indicated. Thus (Figure 7.3), a
detailed display of part of a map can be placed near a global, but necessarily less
detailed map, with the location of the detailed map shown. This may be an
improvement on the situation where there is no context at all, but there is now
a continuity problem: it is difficult to transfer mentally from the edge of the
detailed region to the corresponding point in the global map. You may say, 'Why
not bring the two together very simply by using a magnifying glass technique?' A
major disadvantage immediately obvious from Figure 7.4 is that the magnifying
glass occludes the immediate context of the detailed region.

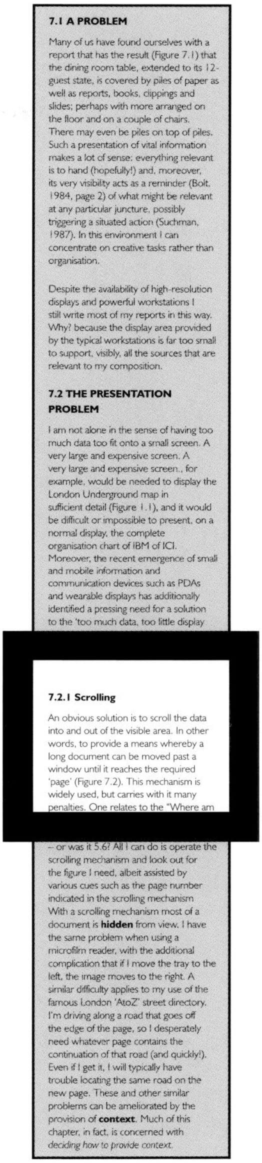

FIGURE 7.2
Scrolling hides
most of a
document

7.1 A PROBLEM

Many of us have found ourselves with a report that has the result (Figure 7.1) that the dining room table, extended to its 12-guest state, is covered by piles of paper as well as reports, books, clippings and slides; perhaps with more arranged on the floor and on a couple of chairs. There may even be piles on top of piles. Such a presentation of vital information makes a lot of sense: everything relevant is to hand (hopefully!) and, moreover, its very visibility acts as a reminder (Bolt, 1984, page 2) of what might be relevant at any particular juncture, possibly triggering a situated action (Suchman, 1987). In this environment I can concentrate on creative tasks rather than organisation.

Despite the availability of high-resolution displays and powerful workstations I still write most of my reports in this way. Why? because the display area provided by the typical workstations is far too small to support, visibly, all the sources that are relevant to my composition.

7.2 THE PRESENTATION PROBLEM

I am not alone in the sense of having too much data too fit onto a small screen. A very large and expensive screen. A very large and expensive screen... for example, would be needed to display the London Underground map in sufficient detail (Figure 1.1), and it would be difficult or impossible to present, on a normal display, the complete organisation chart of IBM of JCI. Moreover, the recent emergence of small and mobile information and communication devices such as PDAs and wearable displays has additionally identified a pressing need for a solution to the 'too much data, too little display

7.2.1 Scrolling

An obvious solution is to scroll the data into and out of the visible area. In other words, to provide a means whereby a long document can be moved past a window until it reaches the required 'page' (Figure 7.2). This mechanism is widely used, but carries with it many penalties. One relates to the "Where am

-- or was it 5.6? All I can do is operate the scrolling mechanism and look out for the figure I need, albeit assisted by various cues such as the page number indicated in the scrolling mechanism With a scrolling mechanism most of a document is **hidden** from view. I have the same problem when using a microfilm reader, with the additional complication that if I move the tray to the left, the image moves to the right. A similar difficulty applies to my use of the famous London 'AtoZ' street directory. I'm driving along a road that goes off the edge of the page, so I desperately need whatever page contains the continuation of that road (and quickly!). Even if I get it, I will typically have trouble locating the same road on the new page. These and other similar problems can be ameliorated by the provision of **context**. Much of this chapter, in fact, is concerned with deciding how to provide context.

The problem of occlusion was addressed by Ware and Lewis (1995) who proposed the DragMag Image Magnifier. The approach adopted (Figure 7.5) is to avoid occlusion by allowing the separation of the (small) region of interest (in the red square) and the resulting magnified image. The region to be magnified, shown with lines connecting it to the magnified image, can itself be panned around the 'base image' independently of the location of the magnified image, which can itself be independently placed. Controls beside the magnified image allow zooming. Nevertheless, the continuity problem still remains.

Another interesting solution to the problem of occlusion is to make the detailed map transparent (except for essential features such as roads and place

FIGURE 7.3
A separate
display of
context

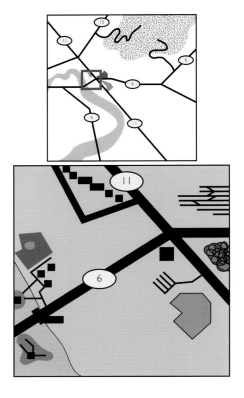

FIGURE 7.4
Conventional
magnification
masks
immediate
context

names), as in Lieberman's (1994, 1997) Macroscope, shown in Figure 7.6. After the area to be magnified is identified (by the red rectangle) it is effectively enlarged to the same size as the original map and then made available for *simultaneous* display. Indeed, a manual control can vary the relative prominence of each map, even to the extremes where either the original map or the magnification of the region of interest is visible on its own.

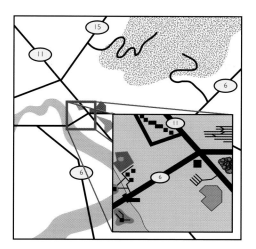

FIGURE 7.5
The DragMag
image magnifier

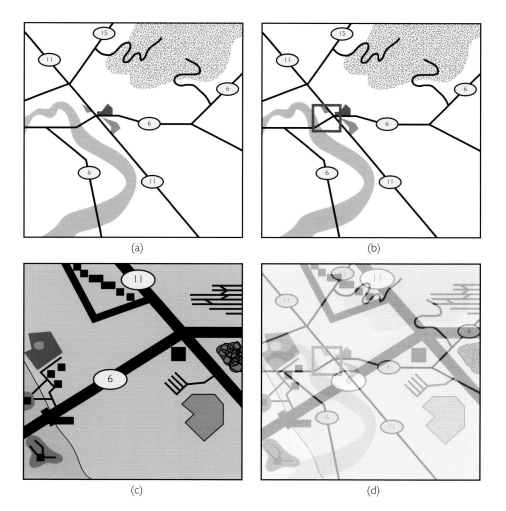

(a)

(b)

(c)

(d)

FIGURE 7.6
Within a large
area (a), detail
within a small
region (b) is of
interest. The
small region is
magnified (c) to
reveal detail,
and then
superimposed
(d) upon the
original map

7.3 Focus+Context

Not surprisingly in view of the importance of context, a great deal of attention has been directed during the last two decades to the solution of the problem created by the need to have context information beneficially co-existing with detail of the focus of attention. One of the most successful concepts, and one which has led to numerous derivative techniques, is the Bifocal Display (Imperial College Television Studio, 1980; Spence and Apperley, 1982).

The principle of the bifocal display is perhaps most easily demonstrated with the physical analogy of a long strip of paper (Figure 7.7) showing a representation of my intray: a variety of symbols represent incoming letters, telephone calls, emails and documents I'm preparing. However, the items are so numerous that this information space cannot be viewed through the normal aperture of a display screen: wherever an aperture is positioned, most of the information space – and hence most of the content (and therefore context) – is hidden from view.

FIGURE 7.7
Representation
of an in-tray

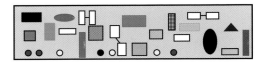

The solution is simple (Figure 7.8): imagine the strip of paper to be pulled back across two posts, but *in such a way that all of it is still in view*. One or two items will appear in the center and, if they are documents, will be readable, but the viewer is still aware of the (albeit distorted) presence of all other items. An electronic implementation of the bifocal concept might appear as sketched in Figure 7.9. This is where the skill of the interaction designer is relevant: if the encoding of the distorted items is carefully chosen, then an informative 'overview' of information space is immediately available. For example, colour might be used to denote the sender of an item, 'X-position' to denote time, 'Y-position' to denote type of communication, and shape to represent extent. For example, the thin red rectangle in the left-most distorted region is a message from my boss: it is readily noticed, and can easily be read if the information space is scrolled until the red rectangle has expanded upon entering the central region. Suitably implemented, a bifocal display might appear as in Figure 7.10.

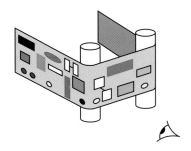

FIGURE 7.8
The principle of the Bifocal Display

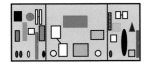

FIGURE 7.9
The Bifocal Display as seen by a user

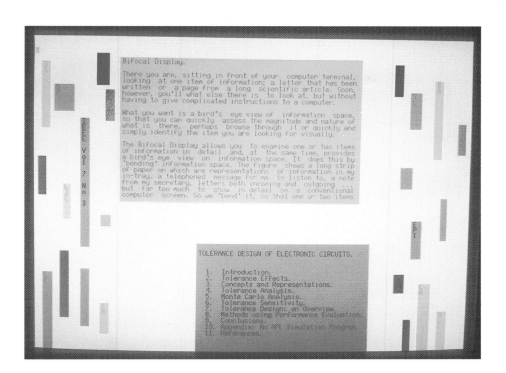

FIGURE 7.10
An early
implementation
of the Bifocal
Display

The bifocal concept was invented long before a satisfactory implementation could be achieved, and was implemented as the Perspective Wall (Mackinlay *et al.*, 1991) eleven years later on an advanced workstation (Figure 7.11). The Perspective Wall simulates a three-dimensional effect, but is essentially demonstrating the same beneficial distortion effects as the Bifocal Display. Other terms associated with the concept are the 'fisheye lens' (see later, p. 120) and the 'distortion technique'.

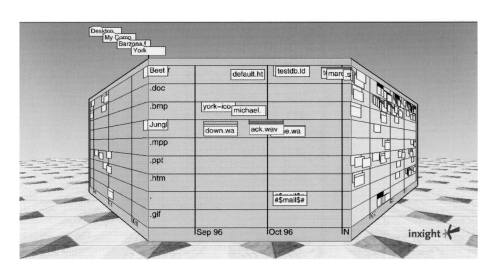

FIGURE 7.11
The Perspective
Wall
Source: *Inxight
Software Inc.*

As illustrated, the bifocal display is based on distortion in the *X*-dimension, shown schematically in Figure 7.12. But distortion can additionally be applied in the *Y*-dimension, as illustrated in Figure 7.13. An example of where this com-

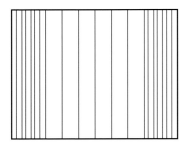

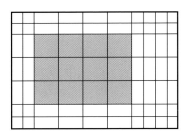

FIGURE 7.12
Distortion in the *X*-dimension

FIGURE 7.13
Distortion in both *X*- and *Y*-dimensions

bined distortion might be useful is shown in Figure 7.14, which is a distorted version of the London Underground map. The advantage over a display such as Figure 7.3 is clear: there is a continuity across the boundaries where the distortion begins, allowing a smooth visual transition between focus and context. Thus, the traveler can easily trace a line out of the detailed region and into the compressed region or, if an appropriate interactive control is provided, may simply move the non-distorted region in order gradually to identify a complete journey. One should not overlook the fact that Harry Beck could be said to have

FIGURE 7.14
The London Underground map distorted in both *X*- and *Y*-dimensions

Source: *Reproduced by kind permission of London Transport Museum*

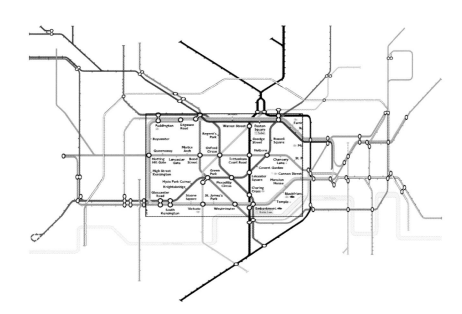

introduced distortion in his original map of the Underground, namely distortion of the underlying geography. Another example where concurrent but separate *X*- and *Y*- distortion can be useful is the diary of Figure 7.15 (Spence and Apperley, 1982): horizontal scrolling *anywhere* on the screen will flip successive weeks into the central region, which *itself* is distorted so that ample space can be devoted, by vertical scrolling, to any selected day. The same principle was applied to the Document Lens by Robertson and Mackinlay (1993).

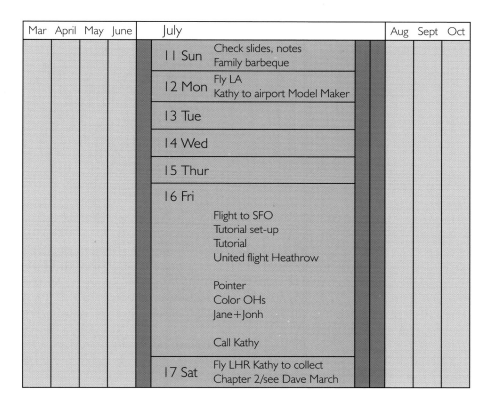

FIGURE 7.15
A diary exploiting both *X*- and *Y*- distortion

The control of a distortion-based display can be achieved in many ways. In the original proposed version of the Bifocal Display concept an item in the distorted region was moved into the central focus region by a simple scrolling action (for example, by moving a finger across the display): hand–eye coordination was sufficient to achieve the repositioning without difficulty. An alternative approach in which the required item is identified by mouse-click, whereupon it automatically moves to the focus region, requires more attention to detail.

The distortion principle inherent in the Bifocal Display concept has also been applied to tables, to allow fine detail to be examined. The Table Lens (Rao and Card, 1994) shown in Figure 7.16 will be familiar from Chapter 2 where the baseball data was seen to be more easily interpreted by interactive rearrangement of the rows. Now, with the Table Lens, detail about individual players can be examined in the context of all the data.

FIGURE 7.16
The Table Lens,
exploiting the
distortion
principle
Source: *Inxight
Software, Inc.*

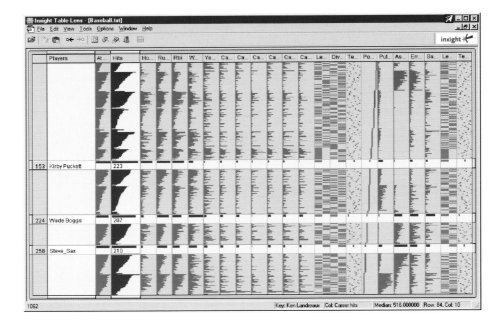

The principle of the Bifocal Display will be familiar to those who frequent poster shops, and especially to those who actually purchase illustrations with titles such as 'A New Yorker's View of the World'. Such a view acknowledges the fact that, to a New Yorker, the postbox, the subway entrance and the corner shop are of far greater day-to-day concern than the entire landmass of Australia, which is therefore given token display as a mound somewhere out to sea. Actually, this presentation involves not only distortion but also suppression, a technique examined in the next section.

The focus+context issue continues to stimulate new solutions (Holmquist, 1997) and applications (Yamaashi *et al.*, 1993) and, in fact, is liable to increase in importance with the proliferation of hand-held information and communication devices, where display area is at a premium. Figure 7.17 shows Holmquist's (1997) flip zoom technique implemented on a simulated palmtop display to function as a web browser (Bjork *et al.*, 1999b).

7.4 Suppression

7.4.1 *Furnas' fisheye concept*

The concept of suppression is perhaps best introduced by an example in which an aircraft maintenance technician is examining the diagram of a very complex mechanism, perhaps in order to rectify a fault (Mitta, 1990). It would not be unusual if the diagram contained far more detail than is relevant to the task at hand, in which case the technician's concentration on the problem could probably be enhanced if irrelevant detail were removed. Thus, the engineering drawing of Figure 7.18 (which is very simple as engineering drawings go!) might be more useful if temporarily simplified to the form shown in Figure 7.19 if some

FIGURE 7.17
The flip zoom
technique
embodied in a
palmtop display
Source: *Lars
Holmquist*

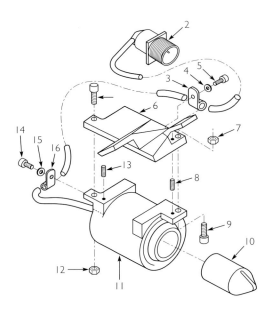

FIGURE 7.18
An engineering drawing
Source: *Mitta (1990)*

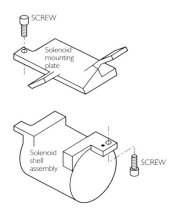

FIGURE 7.19
The engineering drawing simplified
Source: *Mitta (1990)*

system property having to do with the relation between the two screws was of prime concern. The problem is, how do we define relevance, and how do we arrange for irrelevant detail to be suppressed? There are, of course, many different aspects to the relation between two screws, such as their physical occupation of space, the torque transmitted and their shear forces.

A powerful technique for organizing the suppression of irrelevant data was suggested by Furnas (1981, 1986) and called the fisheye technique, a term since used more frequently to describe the distortion techniques introduced earlier. To quote Furnas, the fundamental motivation for the strategy he proposed '. . . is to provide a balance of local detail and global context'. At first sight the motivation is identical with that which led to the bifocal display concept. The essence of Furnas' proposal, however, is that it is often helpful to display data *only if its perceived value exceeds some threshold set by the user*.

The concept was originally illustrated by reference to a tree-structured hierarchical database in which the 'degree of interest' (or *importance* or *priority* or *worth*) of any node decreases by one the further one moves in the tree away from a node designated as the focus. Thus, if the root node is the focus, node weights are assigned as shown in Figure 7.20(a), decreasing by one with each link down the tree. The same principle applies if, say, one of the lowest nodes (which is still a root node of another tree) is designated as the focus of interest: the assignment of degrees of interest is then as shown in Figure 7.20(b). If, as with the two screws shown in Figure 7.18 and 7.19, the situation is such that both the nodes selected as foci in Figures 7.20(a) and 7.20(b) are *concurrently* selected as foci, the nodal degrees of interest are obtained by addition, as shown in Figure 7.20(c). If the threshold for display is now set at –4, only the data associated with those nodes shown in black in Figure 7.20(c) is displayed.

FIGURE 7.20
Establishing a degree of interest
(a) Node weights when the designated root node is the focus
(b) Node weights when a leaf node is the focus
(c) Two nodes are foci concurrently

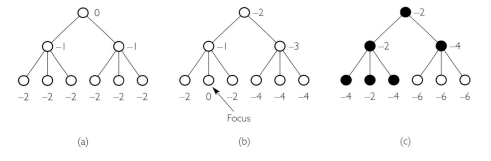

Furnas generalized the concept to handle multiple foci and provided a number of examples ranging from diaries to software. In Mitta's work, shown earlier in Figures 7.18 and 7.19, Furnas' concept was generalized to non-hierarchical information structures, as was the meaning of each arc in the linear graph representing the information structure.

7.4.2 Z-thru mapping

The Z-thru mapping technique invented by Colby and Scholl (1991) also exploits selective display. Here (Figure 7.21) a 'back-plane – in the example a map of the Boston area – can be thought of as potentially being covered by a number of information 'layers', each associated with some feature of the Boston area. Features could include crime statistics, air corridors, weather, obstructions over 2000 feet and traffic density. The user is able to discern information of interest by controlling the focus and transparency of each 'layer'. Here, rather than a degree of interest being assigned within a hierarchical structure, there is a menu of options which can be mixed according to a user's need.

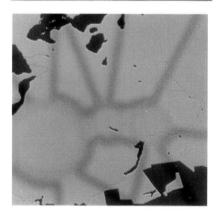

FIGURE 7.21
The Z-thru
mapping
technique

Source: *Colby and
Sholl, Frames,
February 1992*

7.4.3 Mixed techniques

The presentation techniques described above can often be combined to good
effect. One hypothetical example is the 'Really Useful Map' shown in Figure
7.22(a). It addresses the problem of traveling from a hotel in an unfamiliar city
to a relative's house in another unfamiliar city. The presentation employs the
distortion concept, using 'rubber sheet' distortion (Kadmon and Shlomi, 1978)
as illustrated in Figure 7.22(b), to provide necessary fine detail to support navigation within the two cities. It also employs suppression to acknowledge that,

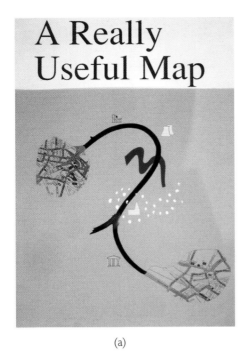

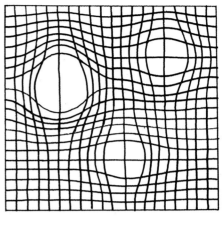

(a)   (b)

once the vehicle is on the motorway, the driver is best served by only the occasional landmark, the sight of which can instil confidence that the vehicle is on the correct route. In this way the map of Figure 7.22(a) combines both distortion and suppression with encoding (Spence, 1993).

To place the concepts discussed above in historical perspective it has to be pointed out that, once the concepts of distortion, suppression and encoding are understood, it is not difficult to identify such techniques in old maps. Thus, in the mid-thirteenth century the Benedictine monk Matthew Parish provided such an example in his map of the journey between London and Jerusalem (Barber and Board, 1993). Currently, attempts are being made to find a formal framework for focus+context tools (Bjork *et al.*, 1999a).

7.5 Magic lenses

Reflecting the message of Chapter 2, we can say that the process of presentation is that of arranging and rearranging the view that we have of data. So far, in all the examples in this chapter, we can observe that a visualization tool has been constructed and that the data that is subsequently rearranged has been brought to the tool. But why not bring the tool to the data? To illustrate this approach, and decide whether it offers benefits (Stone *et al.*, 1994), we first consider two examples drawn from creative writing and house-seeking.

In creative writing one often needs clarification of a word, either because someone else has used that word or because one has used the word oneself without being absolutely sure about its definition. An appropriate Magic Lens

(Figure 7.23) would first be moved from its resting position on the display to lie roughly over the sentence in which the word appears; the word itself would then be identified by means of a cursor; whereupon the lens would resize itself to provide sufficient room for the definition, and the definition then appears. Adequate discrimination must be achieved between the text and the definition, possibly by colour encoding supported by suitable positioning. In this way the tool (generically termed a magic lens) is brought to the data, the latter represented in this example by familiar text.

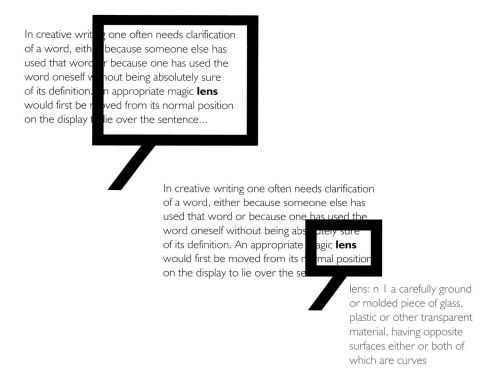

FIGURE 7.23
A Magic Lens employed to clarify the meaning of a word

Why is the magic lens concept a good idea? Most obvious is the attractive metaphor – that of bringing a magnifying glass to something in order to discern more detail. Furthermore, limiting the display of detail to a small region removes the danger of clutter over the whole display, and is less expensive computationally than if the function of the lens were to be applied globally. Indeed, leaving the area outside the lens unmodified provides useful context.

The concept of a magic lens is, in fact, quite general, since it is concerned with accessing the underlying data structures of an application and reformatting the data to generate a modified view. This property, could, for example, be usefully applied to the activity of house-seeking: a different lens, placed over part of a map, could show the images of a number of houses, all selected on the basis of limits set on price, number of bedrooms and other parameters: thus, a magic lens can be parameterized. If space is limited the house images could automatically and continuously move through the viewing area. The lens could alternatively be adjusted to identify the locations of schools and hotels.

A useful property that can be exhibited by magic lenses is that, if they overlap, their separate effects can be combined in appropriate order, thereby offering the possibility of visual macros.

7.6 What's there?

There are many situations in which browsing, as defined in Chapter 6, plays a particularly important part. One arises when a person returns home after a tiring day, sits in their favourite armchair and attempts to see if something interesting is offered by any of a very large number of television channels. How does one design a supportive display to satisfy that need, a need characterized by the question 'What's there?' A similar need relates to a user who has either forgotten what was put in a given folder, or has been given some folders and quickly wants to assess the nature of their content.

One answer is to allow the user to 'riffle' through content, just as one is able to pick up a potentially interesting book, riffle through its pages in a very short time (for example, three seconds) but sufficient to gain some idea of what the book contains. Two applications of the riffling technique are shown in Figures 7.24 and 7.25.

FIGURE 7.24
A video-on-demand system supporting the browsing of video posters

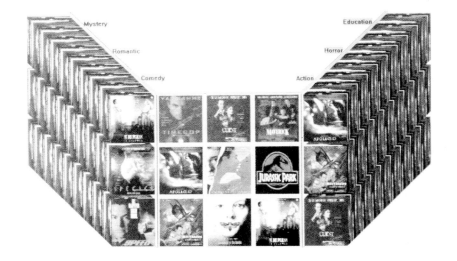

As illustrated in Figure 7.24, Lam and Spence (1997) reported a video-on-demand presentation to support the browsing of video posters. A large number of posters are arranged in three rows on a wall which allows some posters to be viewed 'full face' in the center, but also be 'pulled out' from the side walls, an arrangement very similar to the bifocal display described earlier in this chapter. Movement of the cursor along the edge of the side walls causes each poster to 'pop out' and be fully displayed for as long as the cursor remains at the position of that poster. Anecdotal evidence suggests that display rates of around five per second were satisfactory for the recognition of one or more posters of potential

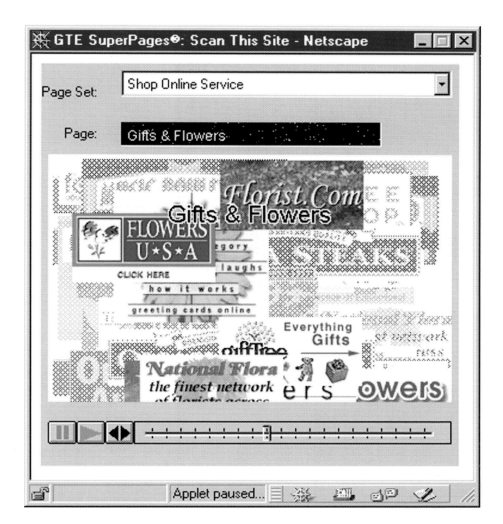

FIGURE 7.25
The presentation of goods and services to potential customers

Source: *AV198*

interest. In one sense the example illustrates a trade-off between space and time, since simultaneous full view of all the posters might require display space larger than the screen. Using a similar principle Wittenburg *et al.* (1998) have described an application (Figure 7.25) designed to present goods and services for purchase to potential customers. As time proceeds, images appear in sequence on the display.

A third application of the riffling technique (de Bruijn and Spence, 1999, 2000) is shown in Figure 7.26. A user has forgotten what is in the folder labeled 'new'. A mouse-click in the semicircular area triggers a rapid serial visual presentation (RSVP) of images of the content, the trajectory suggesting that the images are emerging from one side of the folder and then returning via the other. At a rate as high as about ten per second or more a user is able to gain some idea about content and perhaps recognize an image that is being sought. The black segment will completely fill the semicircle when all images have been displayed, thereby providing some idea of the time it will take to view the entire set of images. A second click will stop the riffling. Other controls (for example,

FIGURE 7.26
Rapid Serial
Visual
Presentation
(RSVP) of
images within a
folder
Source: *GTE*
Laboratories

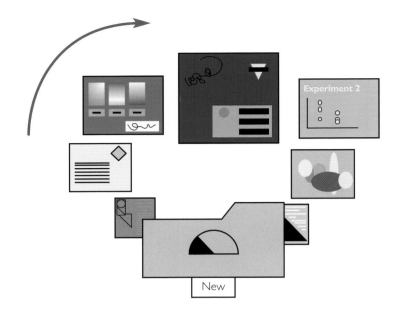

increment/decrement by one) can be added according to the application. Rather than provide each folder explicitly with a mechanism to control the riffling, the riffling function might best be provided by a magic lens.

7.7 Effective view

It is sometimes the case that a constraint is imposed upon the presentation of data by some unrelated requirement, for example by the need of a user to rearrange the presentation in a manner reflecting 'movement' in some information space. As an illustrative example we consider the ordered list of items (fruit) shown in Figure 7.27(a), and assume that the user (who is aware of the alphabetic ordering) will wish to search for a particular item. Typically the list will be so long, or the display area so small, that the user will only be able to view part of the list: in our simple illustrative example the viewing window contains five items (Figure 7.27(b)). 'Movement' through the list towards a desired item is achieved by 'clicking' on an item currently within the viewing window. The number of choices available to the user is called the 'out degree' or 'view size'.

Unfortunately, with a small view size and a long list, the user will be faced with a large number of successive selections: thus, if the word 'quince' is sought, clicking on the bottom line within the window ('kale' in the example) causes that line to appear in the center of the window. Available jumps within the window are shown in Figure 7.27(c). Furnas (1997) therefore proposed a measure of the 'diameter' of the graph in terms of how many interactions (for example, clicks) are involved in moving from one end of the list to the other. For the scheme shown in Figure 7.27 the diameter is proportional to N, the number of items in the list. In the design of such a presentation one would aim to keep both the view size and the diameter reasonably small. For very long lists (for example, a town's telephone directory) the number of interactions would be prohibitive, which is why a scroll bar is so useful.

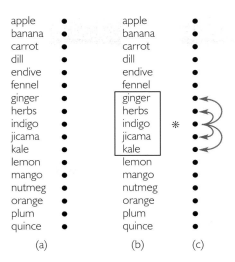

FIGURE 7.27
An effective
view of a list,
and movement
through it

A different view of items within the list can significantly decrease the diameter, thereby reducing the number of interactions required to reach a given item. The scheme shown in Figure 7.28 resembles the bifocal display to some extent because, from a central item in the viewing window, the user can both see and click on items that are at a distance of 1, 2, 4, 8 and so on away in the list: it shows the 'local' part of the list in some detail, and further regions in successively less detail. With this view, movement from one item to another by clicking on a visible item is a process that looks much like binary search (Figure 7.28): indeed, the diameter turns out to be of the order of $\log N$, which is much less than N.

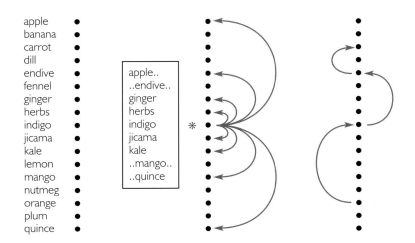

FIGURE 7.28
A rearrange-
ment of the
effective view
to facilitate
movement
through the list

Furnas presented other approaches, of which we shall examine one. If the original list is transformed into two dimensions (Figure 7.29) the view size can be small but show neighbours in both columns and rows. Now the diameter is of

FIGURE 7.29
Transformation
of the list into
two dimensions

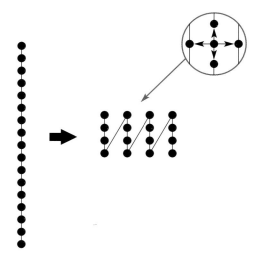

the order of the square root of N. Taking this rearrangement one step further by rearranging (Figure 7.30) the list in three dimensions (much like a telephone directory), and assuming that the view from one page to the next can be supported (by alphabetic tags, for example) then the diameter falls to the order of the cube root of N.

FIGURE 7.30
Transformation
of the list into
three
dimensions

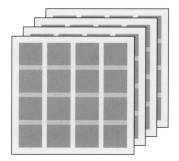

7.8 Zoom and pan

Television watchers and cinemagoers – in other words, virtually everyone – knows what panning and zooming are. Panning (Figure 7.31) is the smooth movement of a viewing frame over a two-dimensional image of greater size. Zooming (Figure 7.32) is the increasing magnification of a decreasing fraction (or vice versa) of a two-dimensional image under the constraint of a viewing frame of constant size. The choice of viewing location afforded by panning, and the ability, offered by zooming, to choose between local detail and global overview, are easily appreciated.

A more demanding requirement can sometimes arise. Suppose a user has completed a local examination of an object **A** within an image (Figure 7.33) and now wishes to similarly examine an object **B** within the same image but currently not

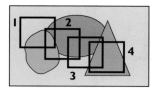

FIGURE 7.31
Panning is the smooth movement of
a viewing frame over a 2D image

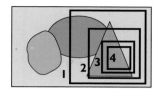

FIGURE 7.32
Zooming is the increasing magnification
of a decreasing fraction of an image (or
vice versa)

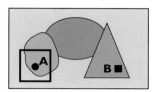

FIGURE 7.33
Transfer of the
focus of attention
from item **A** to
item **B**

in view. A conventional pan would, at first sight, satisfy this requirement. However,
recalling the discussion of internal models in Chapter 6, we would identify the
benefit of first zooming out until both foci of interest (**A** and **B**) are in view, and
then carrying out a short pan in such a way that a subsequent pure zoom will provide local detail of **B**. In this way the user's internal model of the global area within
which **A** and **B** are located is either generated or refreshed. This and other
processes concerned with scale can be explained by reference to the concept of
space–scale diagrams (Furnas and Bederson, 1995) illustrated in Figure 7.34.

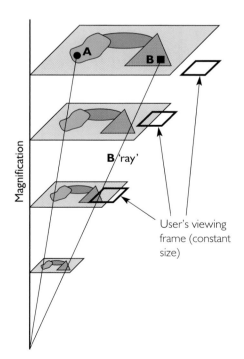

FIGURE 7.34
A space–scale
diagram
pertinent to
Figure 7.33

A space–scale diagram (Figure 7.34) contains a number of copies of a rectangular two-dimensional image arranged vertically along a magnification scale, and stacked to form an inverted pyramid. If image magnification is proportional to vertical distance, it follows that a single point **A** (the black circle in the yellow area) in the image identifies a straight 'ray' passing through the origin. A similar ray tracks the point **B**, a black square within the green triangle. In the same space the user's viewing frame is represented by a square of *constant* size, irrespective of where it is placed in the diagram. Thus, horizontal movement of the viewing frame represents panning, while vertical movement describes zooming. For the process described above – a zoom out from **A** until **B** is within the frame, followed by a short pan and then zooming into **B** – the corresponding trajectory (*W, X, Y, Z*) of the viewing frame is shown in Figure 7.35. A single direct pan from *W* to *Z* can be disadvantageous, as already remarked, as far as the user's internal model is concerned: arguably, such a trajectory may also be computationally more expensive (Furnas and Bederson, 1995).

FIGURE 7.35
Trajectories in a space–scale diagram

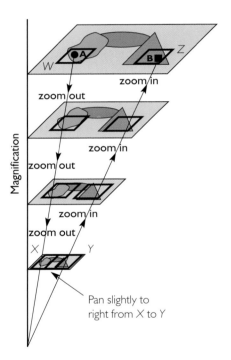

7.8.1 *Semantic zoom*

Taking the zooming concept further leads to the notion of *semantic zoom*. With a conventional geometric zoom all objects change only their size: with semantic zoom they can additionally change shape or, indeed, their very presence in the display. As an illustration we select the Spatial Data Management System (Herot *et al.*, 1981; Herot, 1980) which was installed in the *S.S. Carl Vinson*, and its application to naval operations. In certain circumstances a ship's captain needs to be aware of a collection of available ships (Figure 7.36(a)). In a different situation certain details of a particular ship may be of interest, in which case a

FIGURE 7.36
Semantic zoom

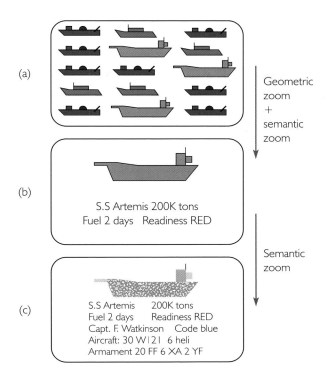

geometric zoom combined with a semantic zoom will provide overall details of that ship (Figure 7.36(b)). Further semantic zoom could display additional information, and perhaps replace the ship icon with a photographic rendition (Figure 7.36(c)). Semantic zoom can also be represented on a space–scale diagram (Furnas and Bederson, 1995) and has been incorporated in the Pad++ Zooming Graphical Interface (Bederson and Hollan, 1994).

CHAPTER 8

Connectivity

8.1 Connections

There is a class of phenomena whose underlying feature is that of *connection*, examples of which can be found in a wide range of fields. Harry Beck's static map of the London Underground railway system of 1931 (Figure 8.1) focused on connections since it was the problem of traveling underground from one station to another, *with little concern for geography*, that was the motivator (Garland, 1994); nevertheless, some element of spatial relevance was still essential. Earlier maps had also shown connectedness (or *topology*) but had allowed familiar geography to be the overriding consideration (Figure 8.2). Descriptions of wars to be found in historical or archaeological texts (Arnold, 1997) are also essentially describing connections, but additionally contain useful information such as who attacked who: here, a simple graphic presentation allows useful visualization (Figure 8.3). In many examples the basic connectivity information is enhanced by parameterization. Thus, SO-grams ('significant other' grams) employed by sociologists to describe close personal relationships (Davenport and Buckner, 1998; Davenport *et al.*, 1998) have a topology as their basis (Figure 8.4) but become far richer from parameterization with regard to the nature of interaction ('we speak on the phone every day', 'we exchange gifts at Christmas', 'we meet every Friday in the pub'). The organization chart of a company illustrates connectedness of a special kind in which personnel exist at clearly defined levels within a hierarchy. Similarly, visualization of the function call graph (that is, connectedness) associated with a software system can lead to the proposal of effective compilation strategies (Eick and Wills, 1993).

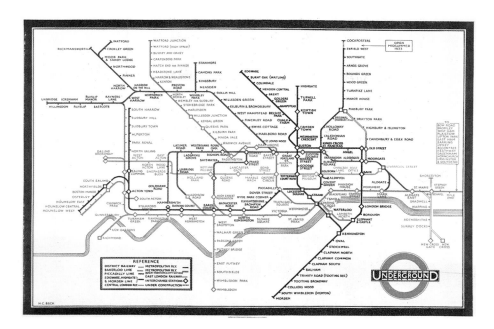

FIGURE 8.1
Harry Beck's original map of the London Underground system

Source: *London Underground Map designed by Harry Beck (1953) © London Transport. Reproduced by kind permission of London Transport*

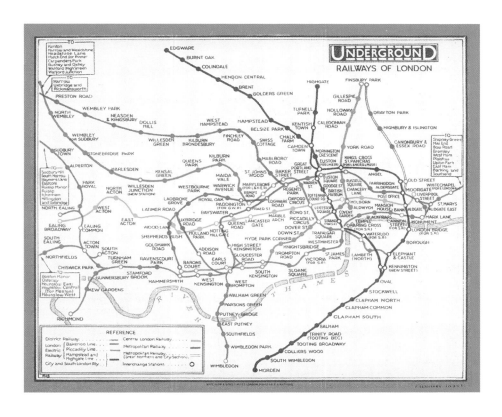

FIGURE 8.2
The London Underground map before Beck's idea was adopted

Source: *London Underground Map designed by H.F. Stingemore (1927) © London Transport. Reproduced by kind permission of London Transport*

FIGURE 8.3
The incidence of warfare in early Anglo-Saxon England (AD 550–700). The red dots indicate the recorded aggressors

Source: *After Arnold (1997)*

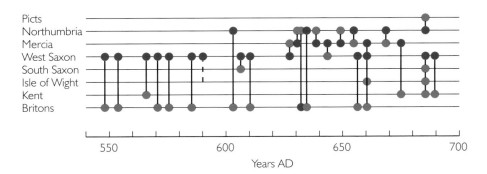

FIGURE 8.4
A hand-sketched significant other- (SO-) gram

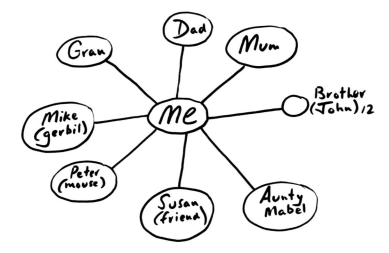

Perhaps the principal current interest in the visualization of connectedness arises from the proliferation of communication networks such as telephone networks, email networks and the Internet. What characterizes many of these applications is their sheer size, a feature which renders the visualization of their structure and behaviour a non-trivial task.

8.1.1 *Graph theory*

A useful formalism for the study of connectivity is that of graphs and graph theory (Bondy and Murthy, 1976), the relevant terminology of which is briefly reviewed here. Connectedness is most conveniently represented by a graph composed of nodes and connecting links. An example from Chapter 2 (Figure 8.5) represented telephone conversations between a number of people: here, nodes represent people and links the occurrence of conversations. The example shows a disjoint graph reflecting the absence of telephone conversations between different clusters of individuals. Such a representation can easily contain information regarding directedness (leading to a directed graph). Parameters are often associated with links. In a telephone network, for example, each link can be characterized by its capacity, by the current traffic density, and by the ratio of incoming to outgoing traffic. Similarly, nodes can have parameters associated with them, such as aggregated incoming and outgoing calls. The graphs associated with modern communication networks tend to be very large and extremely complex, so that one problem posed for the successful visualization of a network and its operation is the fact that its graph can rarely be presented in two dimensions without crossovers and without a danger of occlusion.

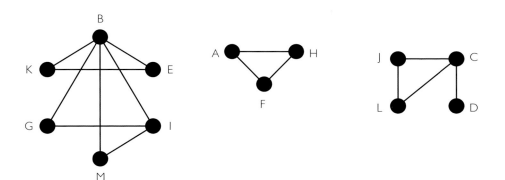

FIGURE 8.5
A network representing telephone conversations

Overall, the treatment of connectedness falls into two classes. The first, which often presents the most severe problems, is concerned with general networks in which any node can be connected to any other node. The second class contains those examples in which the underlying graph is a tree; in other words, there are no loops in the graph. This class is far easier to handle, but is not without challenging problems.

8.2 General networks

8.2.1 The US telephone network

Our first example of a large general network will be the AT&T Long Distance network which is used by AT&T to carry long-distance calls within the United States. Over 110 nodes (called 'switches') are involved and they are nearly completely connected by over 12,000 links. A considerable volume of data is collected, typically every five minutes, concerning the performance of this network. Some data is associated with nodes and some with links. Node data includes aggregated incoming and outgoing traffic; link data includes traffic flow, capacity and overload.

The insight being sought by the operator of the network will determine the appropriate visualization technique(s) to be used. Such insight might be in response to any of a wide range of questions, so we select as our example (Becker *et al.*, 1995) the day of the San Francisco earthquake, October 17, 1989. During this event, relevant questions would include the following:

1. Where are the overloads?
2. Which links are carrying the most traffic?

3.   Was there network damage?

4.   Is there any underutilized capacity?

5.   Are calls into the affected area completing or are they being blocked elsewhere in the network?

6   Is the overload increasing or decreasing?

It is obviously necessary to represent the connections – the links – in some way. An obvious solution is to use line segments between the nodes and character-ize the traffic flow quantitatively (Figure 8.6(a)). Alternatively the traffic flow can be encoded by thickness or colour (Figure 8.6(b)). Any directional property can be indicated either by using two links (Figure 8.6(c)) or by dividing the link into two segments (Figure 8.6(d)). If one of the data values is zero, the division of Figure 8.6(d) has the advantage of being able to reduce clutter, though there may then be some doubt concerning the location of one of the two terminal nodes.

FIGURE 8.6
Representation of links and their parameters

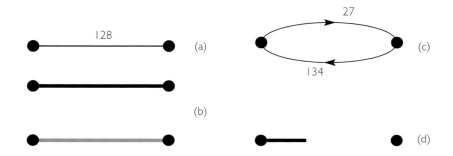

The representation of links is illustrated in the *linkmap* of Figure 8.7 which shows the overload into and out of the Oakland node during the earthquake. The divided representation of Figure 8.6(d) is employed to encode the overload by direction. However, if the same technique is used to investigate overload over the entire network (Figure 8.8), a disadvantage becomes apparent: there are many long lines that obscure most of the country. It is also difficult to see where a divided link terminates. These disadvantages can be ameliorated to some extent by drawing important links last (so that they appear on top) and by using line thickness as an encoding mechanism.

Figure 8.9 is another example of the presentation of connectivity-related data. For a local telephone network it shows, by the (colour coded) size of the dots, talk time within a four-hour period and, by line thickness, the talk time between individuals.

The impression should not be gained that it is a simple matter to choose the parameters which associate node and link quantities with the encoding mecha-nisms. As Becker *et al.* (1995) remark:

> . . . *it takes talent, and sometimes luck, to select the proper parameter values. . . . The analyst manipulates the display parameters dynamically while watching the display change: good parameter [choice] is achieved when the display shows meaningful information about the data.*

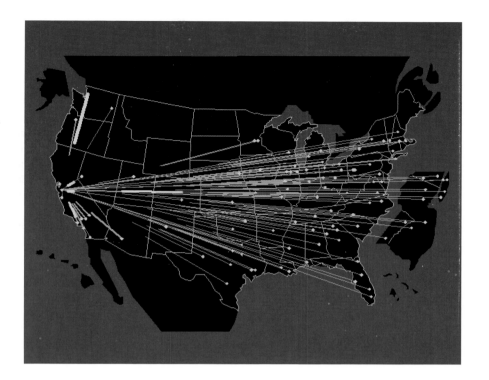

FIGURE 8.7
A linkmap showing the overload into and out of the Oakland node during the earthquake of October 17, 1989

Source: © 1995 *IEEE*

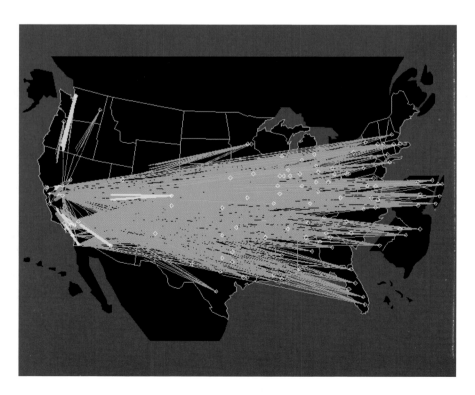

FIGURE 8.8
Illustrating the danger of occlusion
Source: © 1992 *IEEE*

FIGURE 8.9
Communication
within a local
telephone
network

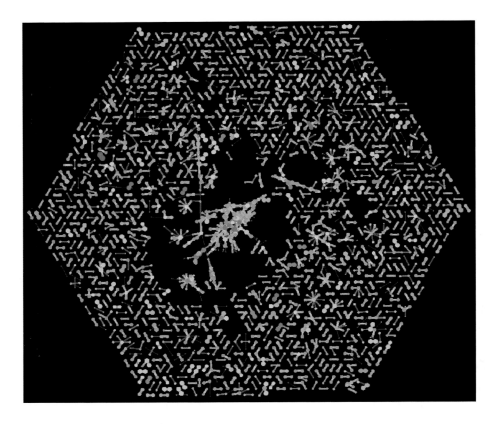

8.2.2 *Electronic mail*

Many visualization issues are common to telephone networks and the use of electronic mail. At a first glance the representation of email usage within a company department, as shown in Figure 8.10, has much in common with previous figures showing telephone traffic. There are, however, significant differences. With email, geographic location is not so relevant: while San Francisco has remained in its current and well-known position for a long time, the location of

FIGURE 8.10
Representation
of email usage
within a
department

Source: © 1993
IEEE

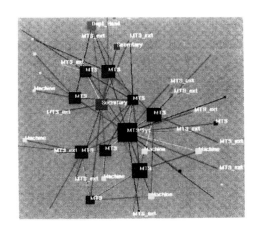

Mr Smith's office is not regarded as of great importance: instead, what is more important is for his node to be so placed within a display as to convey significant information about his email usage. It is also useful to classify different functions associated with the nodes: thus, red represents a clerical worker, whereas technical staff are blue and managers are green. However, just as with the telephone network presentation, node size indicates the aggregated volume of traffic, and links are encoded, in this case using the 'heat scale' – blue for few, through green and then yellow to red for many – to represent volume of email transmission.

The display of Figure 8.10 was generated by the HierNet tool (Eick and Wills, 1993) which offers many functions. An important one is that of placement, since proximity in the display can convey a great deal of understanding: for example the close collaboration between a small group of workers and the lack of interaction between others. Such placement is achieved by 'node placement algorithms' (Kruskal and Wish, 1979; Eick and Wills, 1993). In Figure 8.10 placement was determined according to the weighted links between nodes: not only did this allow certain interpretations regarding interpersonal collaboration but, as a bonus, tended to reduce clutter in the display. The HierNet tool also provided the ability to investigate statistics in the general manner discussed in Chapters 4 and 5, and also offered animation to investigate, for example, the change in personal collaborations over time.

8.2.3 The Netmap visualization tool

Graphs can also usefully represent the connections between people and things and services. For example, if I decide to buy the house at 12 Park Street by borrowing money from the Dodgy Bank, and am professionally assisted in this activity by John Moneymaker, there is a connection, or relationship, between two people, a thing (the house) and an institution (the bank). How graphs representing such connections can provide a useful visualization tool can be illustrated by a particular, and quite remarkable, application of the Netmap tool[1] (Westphal and Blaxton,1998; Davidson, 1993) to the activity of fraud detection.

The Serious Fraud Office (SFO) of the United Kingdom recently spent eight person years examining 48 file drawers of data in order to identify the perpetrator of a suspected building society fraud. An alleged perpetrator was identified, sent for trial and judged guilty. The same task was then set to a single investigator provided with the Netmap visualization tool which, in turn, had access to the same data. The same alleged perpetrator was identified within four weeks! What is more, the Netmap software made it possible, at the same time, to additionally identify the person who was behind the fraud.

The basic Netmap display has the form shown in Figure 8.11. Within an annulus, groups of radial segments are associated with similar entities; in the fraud example these include money lenders ('lenders'), house buyers ('applicants') (Figure 8.12), houses ('properties') and house sellers ('estate agents'). The central area is reserved for straight lines which represent connectivity. In our

---

[1] Netmap is a registered trademark of ALTA Europe Ltd.

FIGURE 8.11
The basic Netmap display, with groups of radial segments within an annulus, each segment associated with a particular person or institution or object
Source:
http://www.altaeurope.com

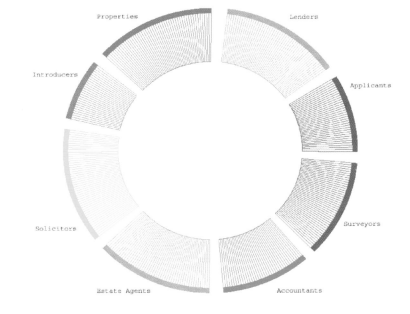

FIGURE 8.12
Detail of segments within a Netmap display
Source:
http://www.altaeurope.com

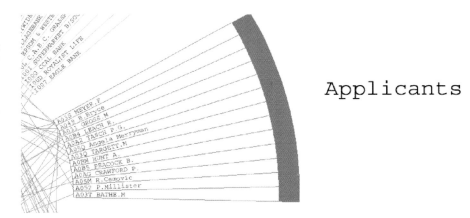

example there would be a straight line connecting the segment representing me, as an applicant, to the segment representing 12 Park Street: other straight lines would represent the other connections involved. If all the lines representing all the connections involved in the fraud case are displayed (Figure 8.13) in the central area, little if any pattern is discernible. However, it is possible to set a threshold so that the only lines displayed are those for which an item is connected to at least three other items (Figure 8.14), whereupon a pattern begins to emerge.

The investigator can now focus on a small subset of the database likely to show fraudulent activity, since it is unlikely that an individual would have more than three applications for a mortgage on a single house. The pattern involves Archer (an introducer, indicated by *), two estate agents called Barker (indicated by +) and Merriman (indicated by #), and a Building Society

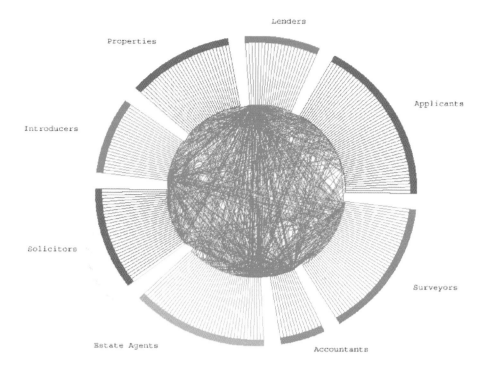

FIGURE 8.13
Lines in the interior of the Netmap display represent connections between items

Source:
http://www.altaeurope.com

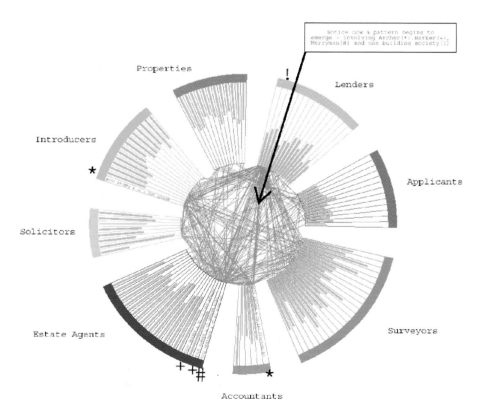

FIGURE 8.14
A threshold of three connections to a single item begins to show a pattern

Source:
http://www.altaeurope.com

(indicated by !).[2] Based on the selected threshold, strongly interconnected items can now be brought together (Figure 8.15) by a clustering algorithm which groups items having more than 50 per cent of their linkages with each other, resulting in circles, outside the main annulus, which allow the investigator to focus on relevant data. The cluster at the top of Figure 8.15 clearly shows the major syndicate responsible for the fraud, and Merryman's company is revealed as the key fraudster – not operating directly but through two networks, its own and Archer's.

FIGURE 8.15
The result of a clustering algorithm applied to items having 50% or more of their links with each other

Source:

http://www.altaeurope .com

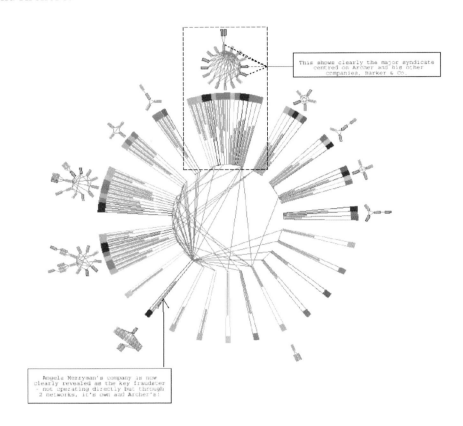

Fraud investigation is just one example of the application of Netmap. By way of contrast its application to the investigation of social interaction within a community (Davenport and Buckner, 1998; Davenport *et al.*, 1998; Connolly, 1998) has been explored. Netmap's displays are not restricted to the 'wagonwheel' form shown in Figures 8.11 to 8.15. For example, the 'step-link' facility supports the ability to group nodes according to the way they are connected (Figure 8.16). Other connectivity-based tools are discussed by Westphal and Blaxton (1998), one of which – Daisy – has something in common with Netmap. Figure 8.17, for example, shows how attributes related to the nodes can usefully be encoded by bar charts within a Daisy display.

---

[2] All names and institutions are fictitious, for obvious reasons.

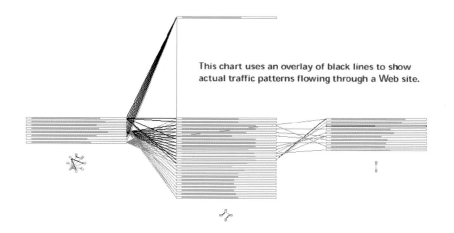

FIGURE 8.16
Illustration of the 'step-link' facility within Netmap

Source:

http://www.altaeurope.com

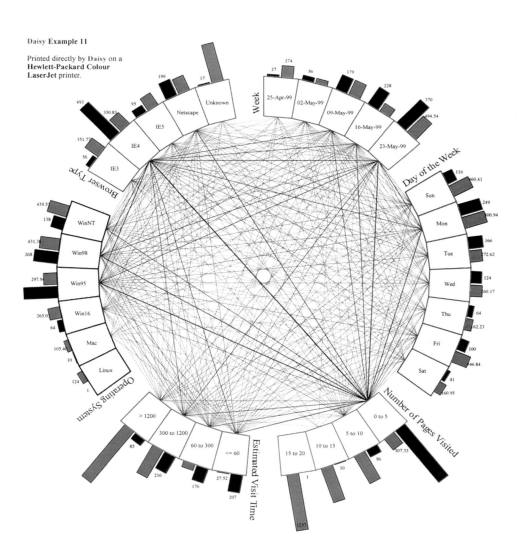

FIGURE 8.17
Bar charts associated with nodes in the Daisy visualization tool

Source:

http://www.daisy.co.uk

8.2.4 *World Wide Web*

The World Wide Web is of enormous size and complexity (Bray, 1996), but is often held up as a prime example of anarchy: its description as the 'biggest car boot sale in the world' reflects something of its character. How big is it? Fifty million Web addresses and rising. How many Web sites? Over 100,000 and again rising rapidly. What about the content? A typical page size is around one to ten Kbytes, and around half contain at least one image reference. How 'connected' is it? Many pages contain at least one URL link: a large majority of sites are pointed to by from one to ten other sites.

From these statistics it is clear that, if the connections implicit in the Web were to be represented by a graph, it would be an enormous graph. So large, in fact, that there is little point in trying to represent or visualize it in its entirety. We must therefore consider the underlying motivation for Web visualization and, thereby, discover what visualization techniques can be of value (Hendley *et al.*, 1995).

Broadly speaking there are two classes of people who might wish to visualize aspects of the Web. One group has much in common with the telecommunication network specialists who employ displays such as those of Figures 8.7 to 8.9 in order to manage and understand global aspects of telephone traffic better. The group would, for example, include website administrators concerned with a site's effectiveness: they would ask questions such as 'Are people entering my site in the way I had imagined?', 'How are people getting to my site?' and 'What is the average path length to a particular node?'. Displays to support appropriate visualization would have much in common with those employed by telecommunication network specialists.

Web users

The other group for whom Web visualization is crucial are Web users, a truly enormous population. As suggested by Chapter 6, the basic reason for movement from one page to another can vary. The motivation may, for example, be to browse with a view to forming a cognitive collage (Figure 8.18) or, and perhaps concurrently, to search for either a well- or poorly-defined target (Figure 8.19). We do, however, know something of their Web traversal habits (Tauscher and Greenberg, 1997). For example, for a wide variety of reasons, the probability that the next page visited has previously been seen is about 58 per cent. This strongly suggests that, to ease a user's task, a display of their past trajectory (called a trace) would be useful, especially if a single direct interaction could

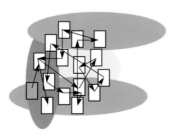

FIGURE 8.18
Browsing to form a cognitive collage

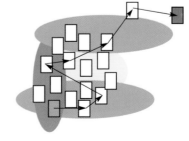

FIGURE 8.19
Search for a target

transfer them back to a previously visited page. Such *selective retreat* (selective revisitation), together with a display of trace (that is, previous nodes visited) was, in fact, found by Field and Apperley (1990) to be a valuable feature of conventional hierarchical menu search: these features were considered, on the basis of experimental evidence, to provide the user with an improved internal model that eased later use of the same menu structure.

Mendelzon (1996) has pointed out the value of a presentation of trace, especially if that presentation offers direct selection to effect transition to a page visited earlier. In fact, a graphical representation (Figure 8.20) of a past trajectory can be enriched considerably by using colour, position, size and arrow direction – to name only a few techniques – to encode such parameters as node dwell-time, bookmarking, revisitation and sequence. Such a facility has other advantages. As well as recognizing that a display of trace with selective retreat reduces a user's cognitive and physical burdens, Tauscher and Greenberg (1997) point out that 'they decrease resource usage by supplanting search engines for finding old pages, and by eliminating navigation through intermediate pages en route to the destination'.

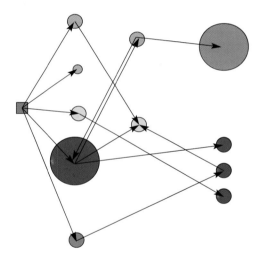

FIGURE 8.20
A display of trace, with retreat to an earlier page achieved by direct selection

A display of trace is also expected to be of value following movement, towards a target, that has been automated by a search query (Figure 8.21). Here, the user is teleported a long (semantic) distance and then requires a localized search to find a target which may only be a few links away: local trace would be helpful. Such 'query initiated browsing' (Furnas 1997) is an emerging paradigm on the Web, and will require appropriate visualization techniques.

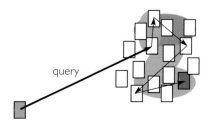

query

FIGURE 8.21
Finding an item of information: query initiated browsing

'Where can I go now?'

'Where am I?' and 'Where have I been?' are not the only important questions asked by the Web user. Especially if they have an intended destination or problem in mind, they also ask 'Where can I (usefully) go from here?'. If the computer is given no hint as to the user's needs (that is, if no query facility is used), it can only provide some indication of which destinations can be reached from the current page. Such an indication can be useful either as context to enhance the user's internal model of their current location or because a move to one of the destinations might bring the user closer to a desired page. Such a 'look ahead' facility was in fact investigated in the context of textual hierarchical menus by Snowberry *et al.* (1985) and found to be instrumental in success in arriving quickly at a required leaf node, suggesting that a look-ahead facility may also be found valuable by Web users.

A number of visualization tools are available to provide 'look ahead' information. A sketch illustrating one possibility is shown in Figure 8.22. Here the concept of a 'bubble' (Boardman, 1995, 2000) is used to represent a page: a bubble can be 'blown' to conceal all inner detail, or 'burst' to display link destinations. Selection of a link destination could automatically blow the current bubble to conceal its contents and take the user to the selected page. Retreat to an earlier page will burst that bubble and disclose its own link destinations. In this way a display of trace and the facilities of selective retreat and look-ahead are combined in a single visualization tool. There are many opportunities for encoding links and bubbles, and rendering them sensitive to interaction, in a display such as Figure 8.22.

Where *should* I go?

Once aware of possible next steps, the question as to which a user should take to satisfy some intention must be answered, and hopefully supported by visualization. In current practice, the Web user makes a subjective assessment based on a – perhaps cursory – examination of the available links, and makes a decision about which page to visit next. An alternative approach, though a challenging one for the visualization tool designer, is to provide, *within what is directly visible*, some clue or 'scent' (Pirolli, 1997) indicating in more or less detail what is available by selecting a particular page; in other words, some sensitivity measure. Such provision is difficult within an essentially anarchic information structure such as the Web. On the other hand, within a well administered and managed structure such as an intranet it might be possible, through the use of coding techniques such as those discussed in Chapter 4, to provide such scent. In conventional menu systems the administrator attempts to provide scent through the appropriate choice of category labels. In the browsing of a very large text collection (Pirolli, 1997) scent was provided automatically by an analysis of available texts. An interesting variant of the concept of scent is that of 'footprints' (Wexelblat and Maes, 1999) descriptive of popular paths explored by others, and which could easily be represented in a display such as that of Figure 8.22.

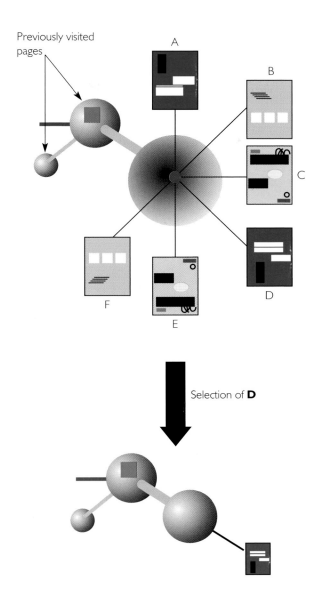

FIGURE 8.22
The use of 'bubbles' to form a representation of trace and to permit both retreat and the display of detail

Previously visited pages

A

B

C

D

E

F

Selection of **D**

8.3 Tree structures

Many relations are characterized by connectedness of a special sort, that which is represented by a graph which is a tree. Examples have already been given in Section 8.1. One is a company reporting structure, with the CEO at the 'root' and many others reporting to a single person and being reported to, in turn, by subordinates. In such an example the designation of a 'root node' is not fundamental to the graph but is determined by what the graph represents: any node in a tree can be so designated. Another example is a software package in which each subroutine is called only by one superordinate function. In the case where a subroutine may be called by more than one function, one or more loops will be introduced into the graph; nevertheless, it may still be possible to employ visualization techniques originally devised for trees (Furnas and Zachs, 1994). Nodes at the (conventional) extremities of the tree are often referred to as 'target nodes' in view of the fact that the function of non-target nodes is frequently to guide the user through a menu to a single source of information. Within a tree we frequently refer to parent, sibling and child nodes (Figure 8.23).

FIGURE 8.23
The terminology associated with trees

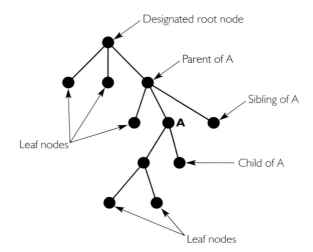

A major problem with trees is that their conventional representation (Figure 8.24) occupies a great deal of space, usually to the extent that for more than three levels and more than 50 nodes at the third level, the tree is too large for effective presentation on a display screen. The search for a better presentation of a tree, and ways in which interaction can be supportive, has resulted in some effective schemes, three of which are now presented.

8.3.1 Cone-Trees

Imagine a 'flat' tree, as shown in two-dimensional space in Figure 8.24, to be remodeled, in three-dimensional space, in such a way that all nodes subordinate to a given node are arranged in a circle which, together with the superordinate node, forms a 'cone' as shown in Figure 8.25. The two-dimensional view of Figure 8.25 is now more compact than that of Figure 8.24 and, notwithstanding

FIGURE 8.24
The representation of a tree quickly becomes difficult to handle within a conventional display

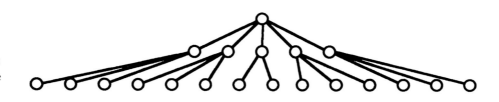

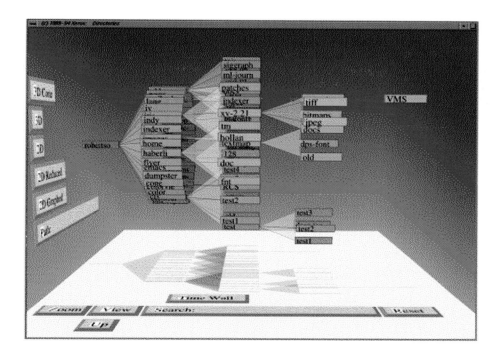

FIGURE 8.25
A Cone-Tree
representation
of hierarchical
data

Source: *Xerox
Corporation*

substantial occlusion, easier to handle. Such a view is called a Cone-Tree (Robertson *et al.*, 1991). The user of a cone tree may, for example, wish to see the reporting path of an employee within an organization represented by the cone tree, in which case entry of the employee's name by some means will bring about any cone rotations needed to position that employee (as well as his reporting path) to the foreground. Following this action, the user might wish to locate another employee to see how they are related to the previous one, in which case entry of the new name would again cause rearrangement of the cones to bring the new name to the fore. Recalling the relevant remarks in Chapter 6, however, we realize that rotation of the cones should not occur instantaneously, and for good reason: a smooth rotation, supported by 'shadows' of the cones on the base plane, supports the maintenance of the user's internal model of the hierarchy. In the words of Stu Card, these techniques 'constitute animation [which] allows the perceptual system to track rotations. The perceptual phenomena of object constancy enables the user to track substructure relations without thinking about it'. The horizontal orientation of the cone tree, shown in Figure 8.25, is also called the cam tree (Robertson *et al.*, 1991) and may be more convenient for the layout of node names than a vertical orientation.

8.3.2 Tree maps

An alternative representation of a tree is the Tree Map (Johnson and Shneiderman, 1991; Shneiderman, 1992). Its derivation from the conventional representation (Figure 8.24) is straightforward and is illustrated in Figure 8.26. The procedure is simple: starting with the designated root node one draws a rectangle; usually, in order to make good use of screen space, it will be almost the same size as the display. Within that rectangle are smaller rectangles, one for

FIGURE 8.26
The derivation
of a Tree Map
from a tree
Source: *Ben
Shneiderman*

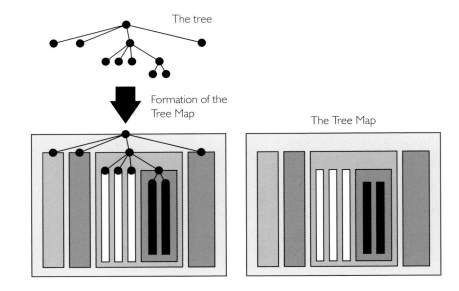

each subordinate node of the node just considered. This construction is repeated until all nodes are accounted for. There is no constraint (except the resolution of the display) on the depth of the tree, and no requirement that all target nodes are at the same level or that the fan-out of each node is the same. Figure 8.27 shows a tree-map representation of baseball data. Reportedly (Johnson, 1993), fifteen minutes of training can lead to effective use of a Tree Map.

FIGURE 8.27
A Tree Map
representation
of Basketball
data

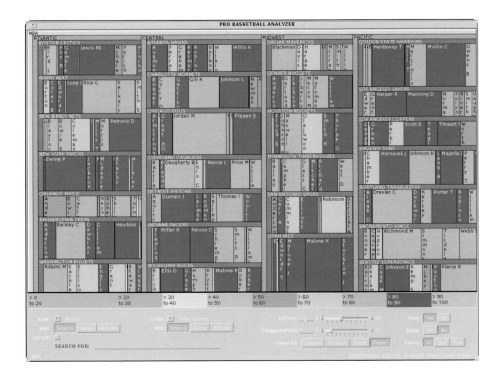

Once derived, individual rectangles can be encoded by colour to denote some attribute: the age of a file, for example, or its composition. If sufficient space is available textual annotation can be added, though the long thin rectangles naturally arising from the process illustrated in Figure 8.26 militate against this. A solution to this problem is available, however (Figure 8.28) and involves alternate horizontal and vertical divisions ('slice and dice') of a rectangle to represent subordinate nodes. In this way a more manageable aspect ratio is associated with most nodes, so that labeling is more easily achieved. An example taken from an author's collection of reports is shown in Figure 8.29.

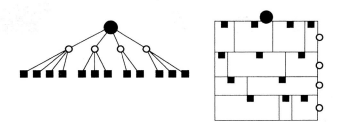

FIGURE 8.28
A modified Tree Map construction with alternating horizontal and vertical divisions

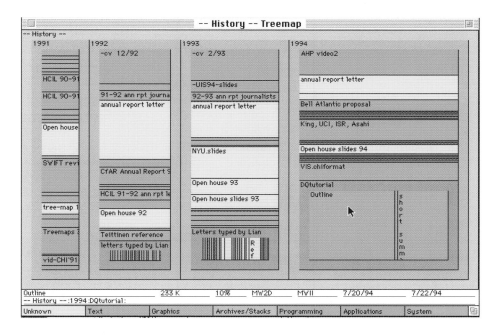

FIGURE 8.29
Tree Map display of an author's collection of reports
Source: *Ben Shneiderman*

8.3.3 Hyperbolic browser

An ingenious technique whereby an entire tree can be kept within the confines of a circular area on a conventional display screen was derived by Lamping and Rao (1994). Without going into the sophisticated mathematical detail involved (Lamping *et al.*, 1995; Lamping and Rao, 1996), the method is based on a hyperbolic geometric transformation with the result that the tree has an appearance of the form shown in Figure 8.30. The designated root node is initially in the

FIGURE 8.30
Appearance of
the hyperbolic
browser
Source: *Inxight
Software, Inc.*

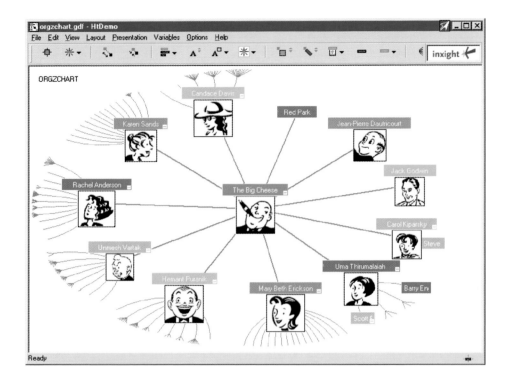

center, with its subordinate nodes arranged around it, and their own subordinate nodes arranged similarly, and so on. As one proceeds outwards from the center of the display the distance between a node and its subordinates decreases in such a manner that, as a result of the hyperbolic transformation, the entire tree 'fits' within the circular area, although drawing of the tree stops below one pixel resolution. In view of its mathematical basis the term 'hyperbolic browser' has been assigned to the technique. It can be said that the hyperbolic browser employs a form of distortion (Chapter 7) to keep the display within bounds and to provide a focus + context view of the data.

Such a presentation has many advantages. Any node which is of interest can easily be moved into the central area so that more detail can be examined. Such movement can be achieved by dragging the node to its new position or by identifying which node should automatically, though smoothly, be brought to the center. With a new node positioned centrally (Figure 8.31) the rest of the tree is appropriately repositioned (as if the node of interest were now considered the root node). An attendant advantage of the hyperbolic display is that a node's context can be viewed in all directions within the tree: its parent, siblings and children are all in close proximity. The mathematical parameters defining the display can be chosen to provide, for the more centrally located nodes, essentially non-overlapping display regions (Figure 8.32) within which details of that node can be displayed or, alternatively, a 'long text' format so that up to 25 characters can be used for each node (Figure 8.33). Indeed, as a node is repositioned, the displayed detail can be adjusted automatically in a 'zoom and bloom' effect, otherwise known as semantic zoom.

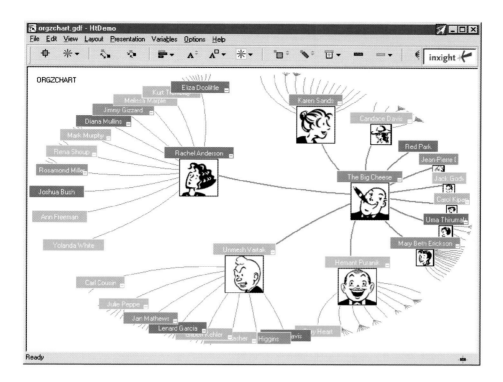

FIGURE 8.31
A new node has been dragged towards the center

Source: *Inxight Software, Inc.*

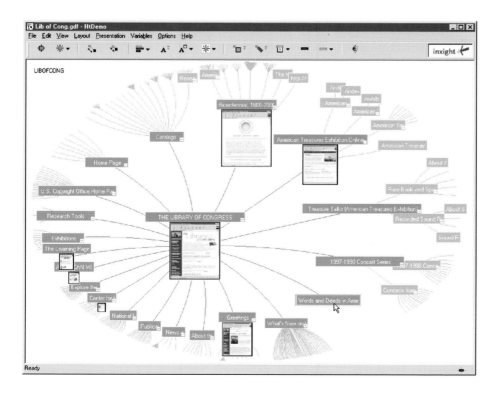

FIGURE 8.32
Effective use of display space in the hyperbolic browser

Source: *Inxight Software, Inc.*

FIGURE 8.33

The 'long text'
format of node
labeling

Source: *Inxight
Software, Inc.*

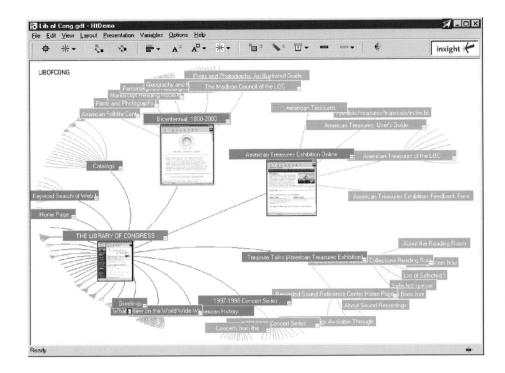

Various extensions and enhancements to the hyperbolic browser are possible. One is a modified transformation that will allow a 'dual focus' presentation, as illustrated by the rubber sheet model in Chapter 7. Another is the use of color-coded nodes to provide 'landmarks' that enable a user to move around the tree (in other words, successively move nodes to the center) with some confidence. Its inventors point out that the hyperbolic transformation is equally applicable to a general graph as well as to a tree, although the 'crossing links' problem would still remain. Many other techniques described in earlier chapters can be introduced into the hyperbolic browser, and will typically depend upon the application. Potential applications are many and varied. For example, the Web visualization tool discussed earlier might place the currently visited page at the root of a hyperbolic browser, with representations of available destinations one link away and their own destinations two links away, and so on.

While the attractive features of the hyperbolic browser can be appreciated to some extent from a written and illustrated description such as the one provided above, a full appreciation of its effectiveness is undoubtedly gained from its interactive use.

CHAPTER 9

Models and Autonomous Processes

9.1 The source of data

With all the visualization techniques discussed so far the data has been *provided*, and the task for the designer of a visualization tool has been to help a user to gain insight into that data. There are some circumstances, however, where data is *not* initially available, and where it is either generated on demand by a user or is the result of some autonomous activity defined and triggered by a user.

An example in which no *a priori* data exists, but where data is specifically generated, is where a civil engineer is designing a dam. Typically, the engineer will employ a simulator which, given details of the proposed dam and certain conditions (for example, water levels) for which the dam's performance is of interest, will generate data whose visualization and interpretation will enhance the designer's understanding. Essentially, this data is generated by the execution of a mathematical model; values of an independent variable (for example, water level) are substituted in the model and the corresponding values of dependent variables (for example, compression within the dam) are computed. The generation of numerical data from a mathematical model is illustrated by the very simple example in Figure 9.1.

The importance of being able to visualize data generated from a model stems from the fact that we possess models for a wide variety of things and processes that we wish to understand and design. They range from models involved in the design of civil engineering structures to financial models relating profit and risk to a choice of investment (Koskinen and Cheung, 1996; Boyle *et al*, 1994; Black and Scholes, 1973; Box and Draper, 1987; Spence, 1999).

FIGURE 9.1
Generation of
numerical data
from a
mathematical
relation

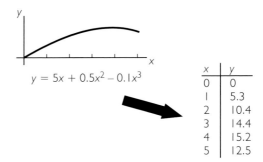

$$y = 5x + 0.5x^2 - 0.1x^3$$

x	y
0	0
1	5.3
2	10.4
3	14.4
4	15.2
5	12.5

Another class of problem for which no data exists *a priori* is where the user merely triggers an autonomous process and then, to gain insight, observes the subsequent behaviour. One example is the execution of a computer program. In one sense the program itself is the model, and when this model is executed – in other words, the program is run – the designer of that program (or a student) will hopefully gain insight into many aspects of its behaviour. A second example is drawn from the behaviour of software agents which autonomously carry out tasks on a user's behalf. There will be many situations where the user will want to visualize agent behaviour, whether it be simply to confirm that the agent is active or to see in some detail what progress has been made, perhaps with a view to adjusting the parameters of that agent's task.

9.2 A structural example

We select a real example to illustrate the visualization issues arising from a situation in which data is generated from a mathematical model. Figure 9.2 shows a structure, about four inches tall, whose function is to support the filament of an electric lamp. When such a structure is being designed, the designer chooses the values of various dimensions (for example, wire width, radius of curvature) which we shall call *parameters*: in the example there are four, labeled X_1 to X_4. These values must be chosen so that, in practical use, the structure performs its function reliably. To ensure reliable operation the designer must in turn ensure that the stresses at locations within the structure are as small as possible. We

FIGURE 9.2
A structure
which supports
the filament of
an electric lamp

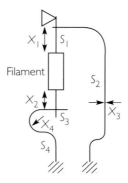

shall refer to these stresses, of which there are four at the positions shown in Figure 9.2, as the *performances* S_1 to S_4. Many other tasks in engineering design have the same framework, as do some in financial design, as we shall see later.

9.3 Influence

The designer's task, that of choosing suitable values for the parameters, is difficult, and is complicated by the fact that the structure will be put into mass-production, a process which cannot be controlled with precision and which therefore leads to inevitable variations in parameter values from one manufactured structure to the next. Thus, in real design the designer must choose a nominal value and tolerance range for each parameter: in other words, a *range* of values rather than a unique value. How can the designer be helped in this difficult task?

Little (and most likely no) help is provided by the mathematical equations which relate performances (that is, stresses) to parameters (that is, dimensions) of the structure, a typical example of which is:

$$S_4 = 60.4 + 23X_1 - 3.8X_2 + 631.2X_3 - 26.4X_4 - 79.7X_1X_3 + 4.8X_2X_3$$
$$+ 2.6X_1X_4 - 2.6X_1{}^2 - 278.2X_3{}^2 + 5.7X_1{}^2X_3 \tag{9.1}$$

The alternative is to examine numerically how the parameters and performances influence each other. Conventionally, at least in the world of engineering design, our interpretation of 'influence' is closely associated with that which can be directly computed. Thus, values of the parameters X_1 to X_4 can be substituted in Equation (9.1) and the corresponding value of S_4 computed. The same calculation can be carried out by one of many available 'simulators', of which NASTRAN is familiar to structural designers. Such a simulator (Figure 9.3) would take a geometric description of the structure of Figure 9.2 and compute the stresses of interest. Again, the influence of parameters upon performances can be computed *directly*.

FIGURE 9.3
In the conventional use of a simulator, parameter values are specified and corresponding performance values are computed

But is this influence of major concern to the designer? In one sense it isn't, because the designer is supplied, by the customer, with desired performances and must somehow decide upon appropriate parameter values. Indeed, it is the 'reverse' of the earlier calculation that is needed here. Unfortunately such reverse influence cannot, except in trivial cases, be directly computed (Figure 9.4). In some cases it would be found that the customer's specifications simply cannot be satisfied: in other words, no choice of parameter values will lead to an acceptable design. In others there may be an infinity of possible designs. Nevertheless, we note for the moment how useful some understanding of the influence of performance requirements on parameter values would be, and return later to show how this influence can be visualized.

FIGURE 9.4
There is no direct way in which parameter values corresponding to a desired performance can be computed

There is a third influence whose understanding, and hence visualization, is immensely valuable to a designer. One example is known as a *trade-off relation*. For example, for a given structure such as the one in Figure 9.2 it may turn out that you cannot simultaneously reduce two of the stresses: if one is small the other will be large, and vice versa. Such a trade-off is extremely common in many fields of design. Here we are looking at the influence of one performance on another performance.

To summarize, there are three influences of interest. One is the influence of parameters on performances. A second is the reverse, the influence of performance specifications on the available choice of parameter values. The third concerns how performances influence each other. Not surprisingly a tool which supports the visualization of these influences is called the Influence Explorer.

9.4 The Influence Explorer

The basis of the Influence Explorer (Tweedie *et al.*, 1995; 1996) can best be illustrated by a simple example in which two parameters X_1 and X_2 determine the values of two performances F_1 and F_2. The parameters and performances can relate to electronic, structural or financial artefacts. First, the designer identifies quite wide ranges (Figure 9.5(a)) of the parameters X_1 and X_2 which together define a Region of Exploration (R_E) of parameter space within which a satisfactory design is considered likely to be found. The choice of R_E is therefore a matter of human judgement, based on experience. Next, this two-dimensional region in parameter space is randomly sampled, typically identifying 200 or more designs (that is, points) within that region. The randomly selected designs are then simulated to establish, for each design, its location (Figure 9.5(b)) in performance space.

FIGURE 9.5
The generation of many parameter–performance pairs by simulation

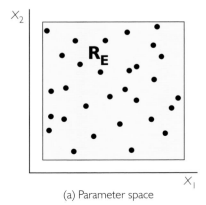

(a) Parameter space

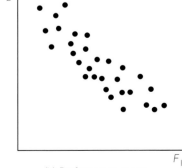

(b) Performance space

Following this precalculation phase the designer now has available a database of designs sufficiently extensive to allow reasonably representative exploration of the relations between the two performances and two parameters. For example, the designer may identify a rectangle in performance space (Figure 9.6) defined by the customer's limits on the two performances and, as a result of the brushing technique introduced in Chapter 3, immediately note the corresponding designs in parameter space. Here is a first exploration of the influence of performances on parameters. Alternatively, to explore the influence of one performance on another, limits corresponding to a narrow range of F_1 can be swept together (Figure 9.7) over the entire range of F_1 and the corresponding trend in F_2 noted. In the example shown the trade-off will quickly be discovered. The advantage gained from precalculation is emphasized in Figure 9.8: the interactive exploration loop typically used to acquire insight now involves no simulation at all and can therefore be responsive in the sense that display of cause and effect is virtually instantaneous.

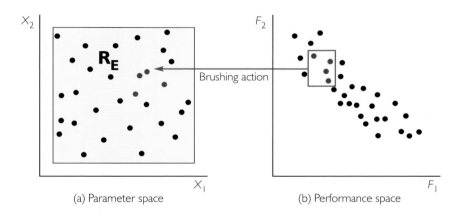

(a) Parameter space   (b) Performance space

FIGURE 9.6
A brushing action highlights the influence of performances on parameters

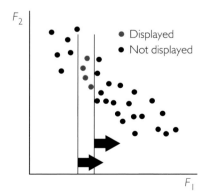

FIGURE 9.7
A swept selection of the F_1 range discloses a trade-off with F_2

FIGURE 9.8
The advantage of precalculation is that responsive 'What if?' exploration is supported

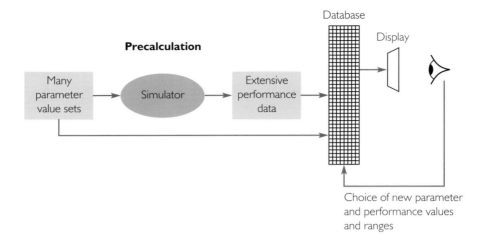

9.4.1 Problems

Despite the simplicity of the concept just illustrated, two apparent drawbacks present themselves. First, the number of simulations is high and, in fields such as electronic circuit or structural design, would conventionally be considered prohibitive. Nevertheless, in many disciplines, simple mathematical models (similar in form to Equation 9.1 above) are available which can considerably reduce the computation involved to manageable levels and render the simulation of hundreds of artefacts possible. One such class of model is called a response surface model (Box and Draper, 1987); others go by the name of macromodels (Boyle *et al.*, 1994) and behavioural models (Koskinen and Cheung, 1996).

The second apparent drawback concerns dimensionality. In real design it is normal to have to consider many parameters rather than two, and many more than two performances. Apparently, therefore, the user might be required to understand the nature of the distribution of a cloud of many designs distributed in two very-high-dimensional spaces, a task which could easily be as difficult as that of understanding the behaviour of the artefact being designed. Fortunately there is a solution to the dimensionality problem; it is to use the concept of linked histograms presented in Chapters 3 and 5.

9.4.2 Histogram approach to high dimensionality

Extension of the concept illustrated in Figure 9.5 to the case of many parameters and many performances is achieved by the presentation shown in Figure 9.9 for the lamp structure of Figure 9.2. This figure shows two sets of histograms, one for parameters and the other for performances. The data presented (Su *et al.*, 1996) is derived from 400 simulations of the structure using mathematical models, one of which is Equation 9.1. Each of the 400 designs is represented by a small rectangle within each histogram, and is made explicit in response to a mouse-click on any histogram, as shown in Figure 9.10.

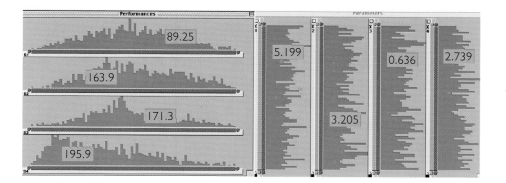

FIGURE 9.9
Performance
histograms and
parameter
histograms for
the structure of
Figure 9.2

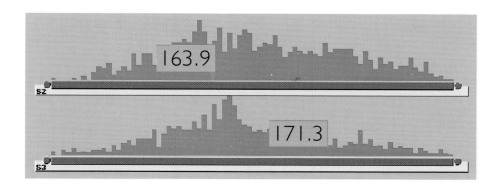

FIGURE 9.10
Each design
contributes to
all histograms

9.4.3 Qualitative exploration

In the early stages of design the designer will probably undertake a great deal of qualitative exploration, principally to gain qualitative insight rather than to choose precise parameter values. One such exploration can draw attention to the third form of influence, that existing between performances. For example (Figure 9.11(a)) suppose that, by adjusting the upper limit of S_4, the designer selects those designs having low values of S_4. As with the Attribute Explorer, the selected designs are color-coded red. It is immediately apparent – because the histograms are linked and brushing has taken place – that those same designs tend to have high values of S_3, low values of S_2 and high values of X_1. It would appear, therefore, that the designer may have discovered some interesting trade-offs and correlations, knowledge of which is invaluable in design. Confirmation of those qualitative relations can be obtained by interactively moving the selected range of S_4 up and down the scale (by simple mouse-drag of the bar between the limits), and simultaneously observing the movement of the red parts of the other histograms: three instants of time during this sequence are illustrated in Figure 9.11(a), (b) and (c). The advantage of such a responsive exploration facility is difficult to appreciate from reading a textual description such as this one, but is immediately and strikingly apparent when actually used. Such visual immediacy allows a designer quickly to discover trade-offs and correlations, and generally acquire valuable insight that would otherwise require extensive and tedious work if only the original simulation tool had been available and no precalculation had been carried out.

FIGURE 9.11
(a) Selection of
a range of
values of S_4 is
brushed into
other
histograms
(a, b and c)
providing
dynamic
confirmation of
the trade-off
between S_4 and
S_3

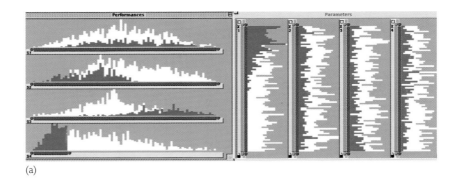

(a)

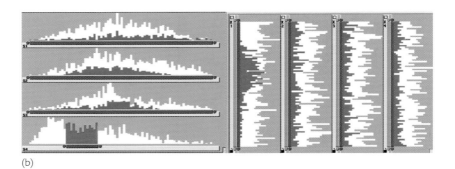

(b)

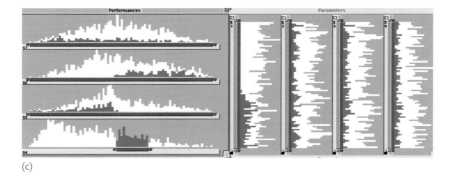

(c)

9.4.4 Summary encoding

In engineering design the number of parameters and performances of interest is typically large, and the question naturally arises as to how many histograms can be accommodated in one display. The approach taken in the Influence Explorer is to recognize that a designer is, at any one time, typically concerned *in detail* with only a few parameters and performances, but nevertheless would like to have an overview of all of them. A solution is shown in Figure 9.12, and uses a technique discussed in Chapter 3. For those variables that are not of immediate or detailed interest the histogram is removed and a yellow dot placed at the average value of the selected designs. Other properties such as variance could

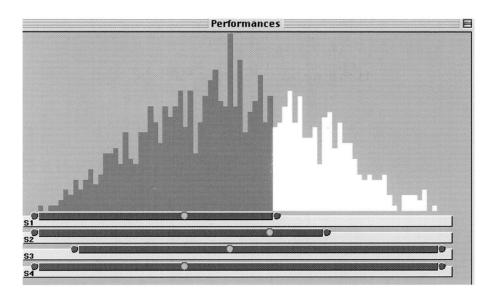

similarly, and equally compactly, be encoded. Any sudden change in the position of a yellow circle would immediately be noticed and, if judged appropriate, the relevant histogram could be restored for detailed examination.

9.4.5 Customer's requirements, and sensitivity

The customer's preferred lower and upper limits on performances are entered by interactively adjusting the limits, as shown in Figure 9.13. As a result, the contribution of each design to the histograms is colour-coded according to the same rules as for the Attribute Explorer: designs satisfying all the customer's requirements are coded red, those failing only one limit are coded black, and so on. Two benefits are provided by this display of 'sensitivity'. First, some idea can be gained about the severity of the different limits. For example, in Figure 9.13 the customer's upper limit on S_2 is quite insensitive in the sense that extension of that limit will only include designs that have *already* failed other limits: no black designs will be included. The second benefit, also derived from the Attribute Explorer, is that if no red designs are shown, then black designs give some indication of the extent to which individual limits must be relaxed to include some satisfactory designs.

9.4.6 Parameter design

The customer's performance limits also lead to similar colour encoding of the parameter histograms: alternatively, the encoding can be in the form shown in Figure 9.14, which only makes a distinction between designs that satisfy the customer's requirements (red) and those that don't (blue). This display is appropriate to the situation in which the design is to be put into mass-production using a manufacturing process exhibiting inevitable variations in parameter values and hence also in performances. To account for such parameter variations the designer must select, for each parameter, not a single value, but a

FIGURE 9.13
The result of specifying acceptable limits on performances

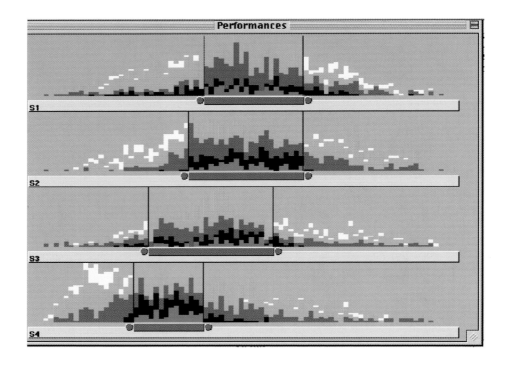

FIGURE 9.14
The distribution of acceptable and unacceptable designs in parameter space, corresponding to limits placed on performances

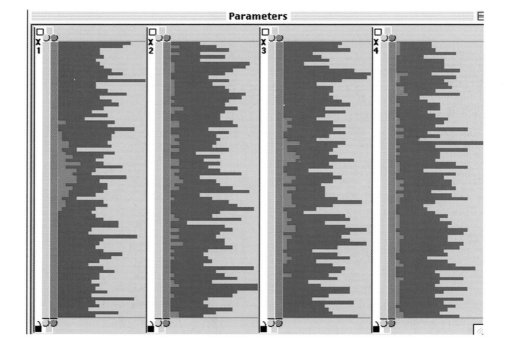

'tolerance range' which acknowledges manufacturing variation. Thus, the designer will choose lower and upper limits to parameter values to enclose as many red designs, and exclude as many blue designs, as possible. More precisely, the aim will usually be to maximize the manufacturing yield, which is the percentage of manufactured designs that satisfy the customer, in this case estimated (Spence and Soin, 1988) as the number of red designs divided by the total number of red and blue designs. The estimated yield is expressed as a percentage and displayed numerically within the Influence Explorer.

9.4.7 Improvements

As design proceeds, and earlier qualitative exploration gives way to quantitative decision making (as in the choice of parameter tolerance ranges), the parameter limits are usually narrowed to correspond to realistic tolerances. In this event the number of precalculated designs lying within the tolerance region will be small and insufficient to provide either the accuracy needed for adequate yield prediction or the encoding needed to guide design. It is a straightforward matter to arrange that, as parameter ranges are narrowed, a new precalculation is carried out to provide an adequate density of designs within the then current tolerance region. In many cases, such a calculation can be carried out in real time as design proceeds.

As a reminder of the complexity of the task of designing an interactive visualization tool for the situation where a model rather than data is provided, a system diagram introduced in Chapter 1 is appropriately modified and shown in Figure 9.15.

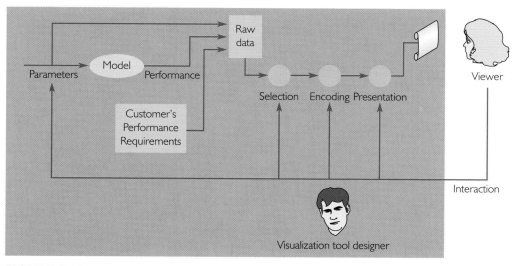

FIGURE 9.15
Structure of a visualization tool in which data is generated from a model

9.4.8 *Financial design*

As an example (Tweedie, 1997) of the application of the Influence Explorer to a field not traditionally thought of as design we present part of a version adapted to options trading. Here the underlying mathematical model (Black and Scholes, 1973) relates, as performances, *Total Cost* and *Profit* to four parameters: they are *Stock price*, *Call strike* (the price at which one would have the option to buy a stock), *Put strike* (the price at which one would have the option to sell a stock) and *Volatility*, the latter relating to the current variation in prices on the stock exchange. A trader will be interested in how to achieve the maximum profit at lowest cost in order to minimize risk. Figure 9.16 shows how a scatterplot can usefully be combined with the histograms of the Influence Explorer to provide the 'strangle curve' familiar to financial analysts.

FIGURE 9.16
The familiar 'Strangle Curve' scatterplot generated by the Influence Explorer from a financial model
Source: *Tweedie*
(1997)

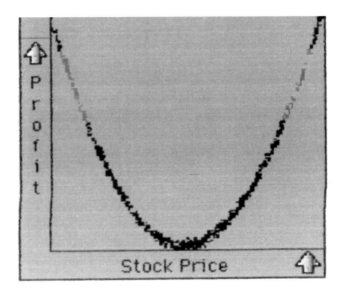

9.5 The Prosection Matrix

The data generated by precalculation (Figure 9.8) can be externalized in a different way, providing the designer with an alternative view of, and potentially enhanced insight into, the relation between parameters and performances. The externalization is called the Prosection Matrix (Tweedie and Spence, 1998) and contains a number of prosections (Furnas and Buja, 1994).

The construction of a prosection is illustrated in Figure 9.17 for the case of three parameters P_1, P_2 and P_3. In the three-dimensional parameter space are a number of points (both black and white – the distinction will soon be clear) representing the parameter sets for which the performance of the artefact has been computed: typically there may be 500 such points. On the P_1P_2-plane the Region of Exploration is shown shaded.

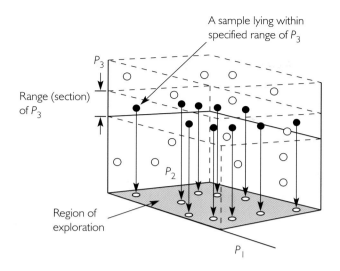

FIGURE 9.17
The
construction of
a prosection

We suppose that the designer has selected a range of P_3 for consideration. This range defines a **section** of parameter space and hence the points which lie within that section: these are the black points. The black points are then **projected** (see the downward pointing arrows) on to the P_1P_2-plane: the result is, for this reason, called a **prosection**. The final step is to colour encode the projections of all points according to whether or not those points represent designs which 'pass' the customer's requirements: typically, passing points are coloured red or green. When coding the failing points it may well be useful to employ the sensitivity colour coding employed in the Attribute and Influence Explorers, and use black, dark gray, light gray and white to indicate a design that has, respectively, failed one, two, three or more customer's requirements on performance.

A typical prosection is shown in Figure 9.18. It is composed of a regular array of squares, the centers of which constitute the population of designs from which a random choice is made during precalculation. The colour of each square is determined by the nature of the sample occurring at its mid-point. What we see in this figure are the boundaries defined in parameter space by the performance limits

FIGURE 9.18
A typical
prosection

set by the customer. Since a single prosection refers to a *pair* of parameters, an artefact described by four parameters will give rise to six prosections: these are typically arranged in a matrix – a Prosection Matrix – as shown in Figure 9.19.

FIGURE 9.19
A Prosection Matrix, with rectangles defining the spread of mass-produced artefacts

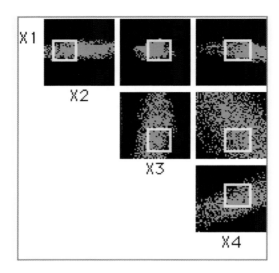

What Figure 9.19 additionally shows are yellow rectangles corresponding to the tolerances on parameter values. In other words, all manufactured samples of the design will be represented by points lying within the yellow rectangles. Thus, the choice of parameter ranges to achieve maximum manufacturing yield is equivalent to the task of positioning the yellow rectangles to lie, as far as possible, within the red regions of the prosections. In this way the prosection matrix has eased a difficult cognitive problem (designing a structure for maximum manufacturing yield) by offering a simple perceptual task (that of placing the yellow rectangles centrally within the red regions). Indeed, it is now possible to identify yet another advantage of the prosection matrix. By varying the performance limits one at a time it is possible to see how the corresponding boundaries in parameter space are affected: it may be the case that a small adjustment of one limit will greatly expand the red region and make the achievement of 100 per cent yield much easier, in which case the customer might be approached to see if this is acceptable. On the other hand, if a performance limit has no effect on the extent of the red region, it may be pointed out to the customer that they could offer for sale a product with tighter tolerances.

Before leaving our discussion of the Influence Explorer and Prosection Matrix it is useful to point out that these visualization tools can also accept existing data – it need not be generated, for example, in a precalculation phase.

9.6 Autonomous processes

We now examine two examples of autonomous behaviour in which no *a priori* data exists, and which is only generated at the request of a user.

9.6.1 Algorithm animation

In the investigation and design of algorithms it is helpful to observe the execution of the algorithm as it proceeds. There are many algorithms whose visualization is useful, and many techniques to facilitate such visualization (Stasko *et al.*, 1998). For illustration here we choose a technique that makes use of three-dimensional presentation and encoding by colour and length (Brown and Najork, 1998). The algorithm selected for illustration is the heapsort algorithm.

The heapsort algorithm takes a list of numbers and rearranges them into ascending order. It works in two phases. In the first, the numbers are selected in turn and placed below an existing number in a binary tree; if the new number is less than or equal to that number it is placed as the left-hand subordinate node, and on the right hand if it is greater. Thus, for the list of numbers:

$$3 \quad 10 \quad 7 \quad 8 \quad 4 \quad 1$$

the number 3 is assigned to the root node (Figure 9.20); the next number (10), being greater than 3, is assigned to the right subordinate node; the next (7), being greater than 3 but less than 10 is assigned to the left subordinate node below 10; and so on until the last number has been added to the tree, with the

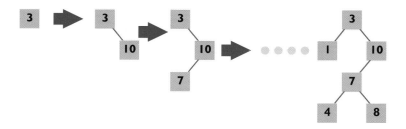

FIGURE 9.20
Illustration of the heapsort algorithm

result shown on the right of Figure 9.20.

In the second phase, the algorithm traverses from left to right from the root node. For example, its left subordinate (1) is added to the new list of numbers. The superordinate node value (3), being greater, is added next, to give the sequence 1, 3. The right-hand subordinate node, of value 10, is found to have a left-hand subordinate node whose value (7) is necessarily less than 10 and, furthermore, that node itself has a left-hand subordinate node whose value (4) is not only less than 7 but is a leaf node, so it is now added to the new list, which is now 1, 3, 4. This process of adding the values of target nodes proceeds until all numbers have been assigned to the new list, which is:

$$1, 3, 4, 7, 8, 10$$

Both the phases are illustrated in Figure 9.21. When viewed from the front as in Figure 9.21(a) one sees a heap configured as a traditional tree (drawn in the *XY* plane). Each node in the tree has a depth (in the '*Z*' dimension) propor-

FIGURE 9.21
Presentation
allowing
visualization of
the heapsort
algorithm

Source: *Stasko,*
Domigue et al. 1998

PLATE II

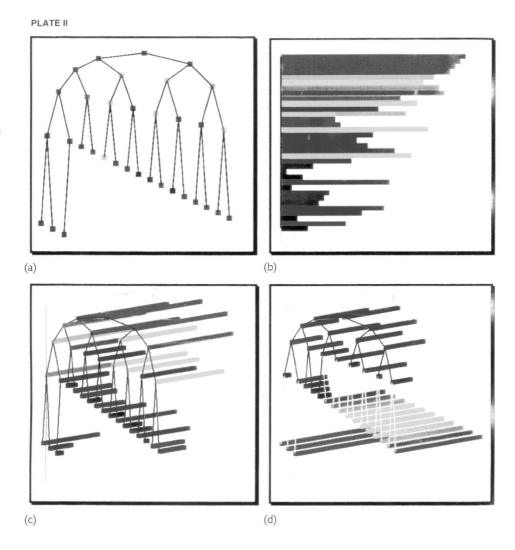

(a)

(b)

(c)

(d)

tional to its value. When the tree is viewed from the side as in Figure 9.21(b) one sees a classical 'sticks' view of the sorting algorithm. Figure 9.21(c) shows the same structure from an oblique viewing angle. When the heap sort is almost complete the display appears as shown in Figure 9.21(d).

The colour coding scheme employs the spectrum, with red denoting large elements and blue the small elements. In one sense colour coding is redundant, since element values are already encoded by their length; nevertheless, colour can be helpful in the tree view. It could be argued that two presentations – the tree of Figure 9.21(a) and the array of Figure 9.21(b) – are sufficient as they stand, and that the three-dimensional view is superfluous. However, in such a case the viewer would have to mentally fuse these two models in order to understand them as a whole.

9.6.2 Agent visualization

An agent is a software entity that acts on behalf of a human being in an autonomous manner, much in the same way as a trusted secretary or agent works. The human 'owner' of an agent is able to define the task of that agent – it may be the filtering of email, the sale of a bicycle or matchmaking to find a pen-friend – and to define the parameters which control that agent's behaviour. For the sale of a bicycle the relevant parameters may be the starting price, the absolute minimum sale price, the manner in which the price should be lowered if no buyer is yet found, and the time limit beyond which the offer should be removed. Other agents within the same software environment may have been instructed by their owners to *buy* a bicycle, again with varying negotiating strategies. Hopefully, but not necessarily, the selling agent will report back to its owner that a sale has been agreed.

The whole *raison d'être* of an agent is that the human is relieved of tasks such as the selling of bicycles and the filtering of email. Nevertheless, there will usually come a time when the human owner of an agent may wonder what that agent is doing, and how it is managing; after all, it is conceivable that the human's instructions are incomplete, inadequate, unduly onerous or based unconsciously upon the premise that the agent possesses 'common sense'. In this event it is helpful if the owner can visualize the agent's behaviour, either simply to make sure that the agent is still active or, at a much greater level of detail, to determine exactly what that agent is currently doing (for example, 'looking up the Yellow Pages') or has done up to now (for example, checked the mall noticeboard, contacted manufacturers).

An example[1] of a display that can allow agent behavior to be visualized to any depth of detail is shown in Figure 9.22. The horizontal lines indicate successive depths to which detail can be viewed. At the top is an animated wheel

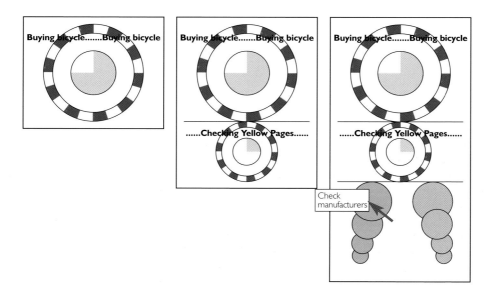

FIGURE 9.22
A visualization tool for gaining insight into agent behaviour at increasing levels of detail

---

[1] I'm most grateful to Sanela Hodžić for permission to use this sketch.

whose rotation indicates that the agent is active, and the inscribed gray segment provides an estimate of how long it might be before a result is achieved. Just this upper wheel, displayed at small scale at the lower edge of a display currently in use for some other purpose, may be sufficient to reassure the human owner. A horizontally scrolling brief textual message may be useful as a reminder of the agent's current task. On demand the smaller rotating wheel can be brought into view: again, the activity and an estimate of the degree of completion of the sub-task are indicated and, again, horizontally scrolling text serves as a reminder of the current action. Greater detail can be unfolded, indicating (in yellow) those subtasks ready to be carried out (and identified in response to a superimposed cursor) as well as those already completed (gray). The extension of such a tool could usefully include visualization of the agent's environment.

CHAPTER 10

Document Visualization

10.1 Visualizing the non-visual

The title of a paper by Wise *et al.* (1995) – 'Visualizing the Non-Visual' – suc-cinctly summarizes the motivation for this chapter. We are concerned primarily with the task of gaining insight into *information which exists in the form of text* within one or more documents, but without reading those documents. A funda-mental issue, therefore, is the problem of transforming certain aspects of a text file into images appropriate to the sort of questions that may be asked by a user.

Interest in this field has been fueled by recent developments in computing and communications. First, there has been a proliferation of documents pre-pared in electronic form, a trend which continues vigorously. Second, a considerable proportion of them are brought together into organized digital libraries and these, combined with a huge volume of (often disorganized) docu-ments distributed around the Web, constitute a huge and rapidly increasing corpus: we are speaking here of hundreds of millions of documents. Finally, thanks to extensive high-speed networks, access to this gigantic collection is available locally. The 'information fire-hose' is on our desks and a mouse-click is all that is needed to turn it on.

The documents of interest can take widely different forms. They may be the texts of news bulletins broadcast on CNN and BBC over the past week, and a user's objective may simply be awareness of the major stories. They may be a collection of scientific papers presented at a series of conferences, and the user may be a researcher trying to locate papers relevant to a new project. Or they may be the collected witness statements associated with a crime, with a detective endeavouring to identify previously unnoticed links that may provide useful additional clues. A quotation which will resonate with these and other users is that of James Thurber, who remarked that

> *So much has already been written about everything that you can't find out anything about it.*

10.2 Queries

More specifically, and usefully, we can identify the sort of question to which the owner of a collection of documents may seek an answer, usually after specifying some keywords representing their interest or after providing a document which is a representative example of their interest:

- Which documents are likely to be of interest to me?
- What other document might be sufficiently close to my interest to be worth consideration?
- Are there any other documents whose title might trigger thoughts that are useful to my search?
- How are my keywords actually distributed in this document?

It is not surprising that many ingenious algorithms have been devised to help answer these and similar questions, but it is equally important to realize that they rarely provide the *whole* answer sought by a user. As pointed out in Chapter 5, there will be many situations in which the response to a question will lead to the modification of that question, starting an iterative process leading eventually to the *confident* formulation of a query and the discovery of a satisfactory answer. Thus, in contrast to the often opaque answer provided solely by an algorithm, there should instead be a transparency permitting swift interpretation, the exercise of judgement and possible interaction. At the same time the displayed output of an algorithm should be compact and informative and, if possible, contain implicit or explicit sensitivity information that will 'point' the user towards a satisfactory conclusion.

10.3 The TileBar scheme

Before proceeding to examine the topic in general we shall examine one system in particular in order to identify the sort of issues that can arise. The system is called TileBars (Hearst, 1995, 1999). TileBars accepts, from its user, a set of *topics* and a collection of *documents* that are thought to have potential to provide insight that the user is seeking, insight which the user feels can be adequately characterized by the selected topics. In the illustrative example of Figure 10.1 the user has chosen the topics 'osteoporosis', 'prevention' and 'research' in view of an interest in knowing more about what research is being carried out into methods of preventing osteoporosis. A topic can, if desired, consist of more than one word, in which case those words would be entered as a list within a single topic. The user must also identify, by some means, the collection of documents that should be examined to locate articles associated with their query: the collection in this example is a set of medical journals.

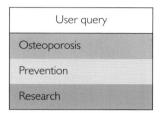

FIGURE 10.1
Specification of a user query by topic words
Source: *Marti Hearst*

For each document in the collection supplied, the TileBars system displays a diagram of the form shown in Figure 10.2. On the left, (but just to the right of a reminder of colours), is the TileBar. It has as many rows as there are topics, and a number of columns corresponding to segments of the document: these may be paragraphs or pages or chapters or be based on some other means of segmentation. By density of shading, each square shows, for the corresponding topic and segment, the relative frequency of occurrence of the word (or words if more than one word is associated with a topic) in that segment. Thus, for the example shown, it is clear that in the first segment (maybe the abstract) there is mention of research but none of prevention or osteoporosis, perhaps indicating that the article will be of little interest: indeed, there is little evidence of the word 'osteoporosis' at all, except for an intriguing segment in which the three topics overlap. Based on the TileBar and the title of the document, the judgement of the user at this point may be to ignore the document 'Recent advances in. . .'.

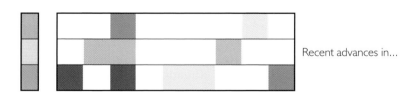

Recent advances in...

FIGURE 10.2
A TileBar indicating the relative occurrence of topic words within segments of a single document
Source: *Marti Hearst*

The appearance of a TileBar screen, for the same set of topics just discussed, is shown[1] in Figure 10.3. If the user judges that the first of the documents investigated may be of interest they can, for example, click on any square to display the corresponding segment, and may choose to select the darkest square (on the top row of the TileBar). The result of this selection, shown in Figure 10.4, is a display of the corresponding paragraph, with the topic words highlighted in the

---

[1] The collection of documents used in the example is the TREC/Tipster collection, provided by the National Institute of Standards and Technology.

FIGURE 10.3
A typical set of
TileBars for a
collection of
documents

Source: *Marti Hearst*

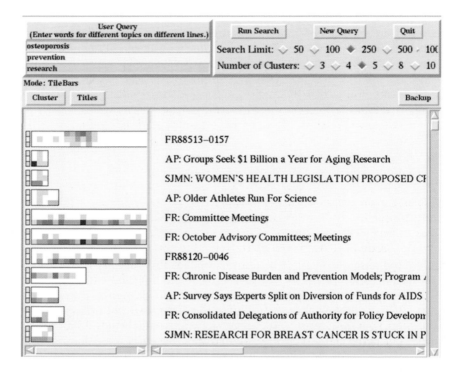

FIGURE 10.4
Display of a
paragraph, with
topic words
highlighted in
appropriate
colours

Source: *Marti Hearst*

<ITAG tagnum=10>Fortunately, scientific knowledge about this disease has grown, and there is reason for hope. Research is revealing that prevention may be achieved through estrogen replacement therapy for older women and through adequate calcium intake and regular weight–bearing exercise for people of all ages. New approaches to diagnosis and treatment are also under active investigation. For this work to continue and for us to take advantage of the knowledge we have already gained, public awareness of osteoporosis and of the importance of further scientific research is essential. </ITAG>

appropriate colour to aid interpretation. As Hearst points out, since the article does not have a title it would have been difficult to determine its relevance without the benefit of the TileBar.

10.4   Issues

TileBars provides, in addition to a useful scheme for document visualization, a hint of the wider issues associated with that activity.

10.4.1 Document visualization is not information retrieval

One issue has to do with the essential difference between document visualization and information retrieval. As Chalmers (1993) remarks, 'the word "retrieval" (Baeza-Yates and Ribeiro-Neto, 1999) suggests an action by some agent to find and bring back information to a somehow detached or uninvolved user. The agent is given a specification of what is wanted, and the user waits for the results to be returned' . He proceeds to repeat one of the main messages of Chapter 5, to the effect that a user may be unable to say exactly what they are looking for in a collection of documents, because they may not *know* exactly what they are looking for. They may initially want to discover *roughly* what is available in the collection and then, by exploration, gradually refine their inquiry.

10.4.2 Keyword ambiguity

A related issue is that of the dialog between user and visualization tool. Many users do not even feel comfortable supplying key words to characterize topics, and may prefer instead to begin by providing or selecting two or three documents as examples of the 'sort of thing' they are looking for, and then proceeding by implicitly redefining their needs by selecting the best of a set of documents. Even if the topics are defined by keywords problems can arise. An obvious example is provided by the words 'gas' and 'petrol', used by inhabitants of the USA and UK respectively to describe the same substance. In fact, a study (Barnard, 1991) showed that the likelihood of any two people using the same name to refer spontaneously to the same concept ranged from 0.07 to 0.18 (that is, 7 to 18 per cent)! However, a related study (Furnas *et al.*, 1983) showed that retrieval success could be dramatically improved by 'multiple aliasing' where a system – like TileBars – can accept many names for the same concept. The case for some access to a dictionary of synonyms is at least established.

10.4.3 Dimensionality

In many schemes for document visualization a single document is characterized by a very large set of numbers: there may be thousands of them, each denoting the frequency of occurrence of a single word in that document (Figure 10.5). Such a representation is predicated upon the assumption that thematic similarity can

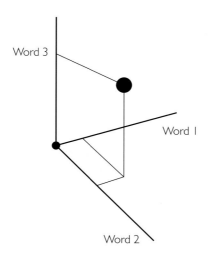

FIGURE 10.5
A point in multidimensional space represents, for a single document, the frequency of occurrence of particular words

be estimated by similarities in word usage. Furthermore, some of these numbers may be weighted (that is, multiplied by some constant) according to whether they are regarded as keywords, perhaps drawn from the document's abstract. We therefore have the problem of evaluating the relevance of perhaps tens or hundreds of documents, each described by an ordered collection of perhaps thousands of numbers. A major issue, therefore, is dimensionality, for there is no way that a human being can visualize a space of many hundreds of dimensions.

As Chalmers (1993) points out, we are used to a three-dimensional space in which we find it easy to perceive and remember the spatial distribution of objects. To be more precise, we are more familiar with horizontal ('X–Y') distributions and patterns than vertical details, so that it might be useful to represent information of interest in '2.5D' space, and to arrange that spatial proximity of document representations corresponds to similarity in the more abstract framework associated with documents. In fact, as discussed in Chapter 2, Chalmers (1993) devised a landscape display in which documents are laid out according to their similarity.

10.4.4 Context

It almost goes without saying that a tool intended to support document visualization should display sufficient content to provide a context within which different documents can be compared and assessed. Like Chalmers we quote Bertin's (1981) remark that

> *Items of data do not supply the information necessary for decision-making. What must be seen are the relationships which emerge from consideration of the entire set of data. In decision-making the useful information is drawn from the overall relationships of the entire set.*

10.5 A general scheme

Most schemes for document visualization have the structure shown in Figure 10.6. First, *Analysis* extracts the essential descriptors of a collection of text, usually according to the interests of a user expressed as a set of key words. In the TileBars example the simple descriptor was the relative occurrence of a word or words in a segment of text. In general, these descriptors may be first-order statistics (such as frequency-based measurements) or higher-order statistics (of interest when a number of documents are being compared) or semantic data capturing aspects of the meaning of the documents. Overall, the output of the analysis stage is a 'shorthand' representation of the original documents – the sets of numbers which form the basis of efficient representation and manipulation by the succeeding stages. Since the analysis stage operates on pure text – by which we mean a written alphabetical form of natural language – we shall assume that any document additionally containing images and tables and diagrams has had those and the pointers to them removed. We also assume the prior removal of common words such as 'a', 'the' and 'some'.

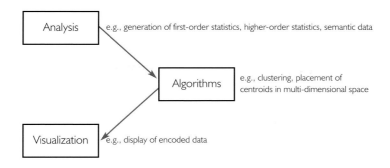

FIGURE 10.6
Stages involved
in many
schemes for
document
visualization

Next, appropriate *algorithms* generate an efficient and flexible representation of documents. As already remarked, the analysis stage may provide, for each of many documents, a vector of as many as 10,000 numbers (Figure 10.5), each corresponding to the frequency of occurrence of a word (one of 10,000 such words automatically identified as possibly significant). Such a representation (Figure 10.7(a)) in a very high-dimensional space, totally unsuitable for visualization purposes, may be transformed, first by *clustering* and then by *projection* into a two- or three-dimensional space (Figure 10.7(b), (c), and (d)).

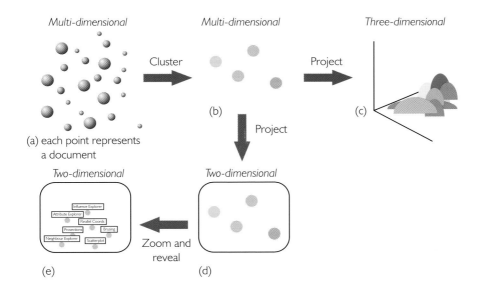

FIGURE 10.7
Clustering and
projection
involved in
document
visualization

The third stage – though often not the *final* stage in view of the advantages of iteration – concerns the manner in which the data produced by the algorithm(s) is *encoded* and *presented* and made *sensitive* to interaction. In the TileBars scheme the third stage (Figure 10.3) presented the TileBars and document titles and allowed the user to 'dig deeper' into selected segments (Figure 10.7 (e)).

With reference to the stages identified in Figure 10.6, but with a focus on the third stage because it directly supports information visualization, we now examine a variety of schemes for document visualization.

10.5.1 Galaxies

As explained, the output of the analysis stage can be a number of vectors of extremely high dimension. For example (Wise *et al.* 1995), suppose that two documents are supplied. The analysis stage will form, for each document, a (usually very high dimensional) vector of these words, and will then examine each document to assign, to each word, a quantitative measure of its frequency of occurrence. One of the two documents may well be a reference document judged by the user to be representative of the sort of content they are seeking: indeed, the user may *prefer* to identify a document rather than a set of topics and keywords.

The analysis stage may then, for example, compute a single measure of similarity between the documents provided. In mathematical parlance this could involve computing the 'inner product' of the two vectors. In other words, it adds up a number of quantities, each obtained by multiplying the frequency of occurrence of a particular word in one document with its corresponding frequency in the second document. This single quantity represents 'query similarity' (Salton *et al.*, 1995). It would then be up to the user to judge, from this single number, whether further investigation into a particular document is potentially worthwhile, perhaps by using the TileBars tool.

The algorithm stage might then perform a clustering process,[2] also identifying the centroid of each cluster (Figure 10.7(b)) to reduce the number of items to be presented visually to a user. The cluster can now be projected to permit visualization. Projection onto two dimensions (Figure 10.7(d)) shows a **Galaxy** of clusters, with provision for the user to interactively dig deeper into any one cluster (Figure 10.7(e)). In view of the possible importance of date of origin a 'temporal slicer' can be valuable: this tool refers to document timestamps and thereby partitions the documents into temporal units which could be anything from minutes to years. Animation might then reveal interesting features.

10.5.2 Themescapes

The projection of a multidimensional cluster can also generate (Figure 10.7(c)) a three-dimensional landscape, one form of which is called a themescape (Wise *et al.*, 1995). A themescape is a 'thematic terrain' that communicates the primary themes of a collection of documents and the relative prevalence of those themes. Elevation in a themescape is a measure of theme strength. The example shown in Figure 10.8 refers to 700 articles relating to the financial industry.

The facilities available to a themescape user are illustrated in Figure 10.9(a) to 10.9(d). In a themescape, documents are represented by small points (Figure 10.9(a)), and those with similar content are placed close together. Peaks appear when there is a concentration of closely related documents. The valleys between peaks can be interesting because they contain fewer documents and more unique content. Topic labels reflect the two or three topics represented in a given area of the map.

---

[2] See York and Bohn (1995) for more detailed discussion of clustering and metric issues.

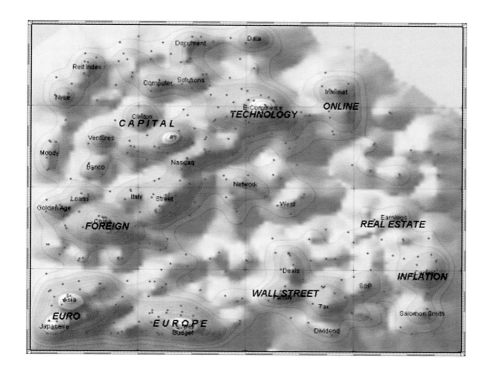

FIGURE 10.8
A themescape
of articles
related to the
financial
industry

Source:
www.cartia.com

Within the landscape metaphor, 'drilling down' to obtain more detail can begin by moving a focus circle (Figure 10.9(b)) to a location of interest: after a slight delay a brief list of the principal topics contained within the circle will appear. Further interaction (Figure 10.9(c)) will display a list of the titles of the documents within the circle; pausing on a title reveals a short summary, while clicking on it causes the document to be opened in a new window.

Once a themescape has been generated a user can make a query either by entering one or more keywords or by selecting words from a list discovered by the internal algorithms. The documents identified by such a query appear on the themescape with numbered dots representing the top documents. The dots so identified can be investigated by the focus circle shown in Figure 10.9(b).

In many situations in which a number of items are being explored it will be desirable to 'flag' those items which may be of interest later. To support this activity flags (Figure 10.9(d)) can be placed on the terrain, and a facility is provided to make summaries of flagged documents.

An advantage of the themescape is that its landscape metaphor and associated drilling down and flagging operations call upon innate human abilities for pattern recognition and spatial reasoning. Another advantage is that it applies equally to single paragraphs and collections of documents.

10.5.3 Galaxy of News

A very different approach to document visualization is embodied in the Galaxy of News system (Rennison, 1994). Users move in three-dimensional space, but in a smooth and continuous fashion rather than in discrete and predetermined

FIGURE 10.9
Facilities
available to a
themescape
user

Source:

www.cartia.com

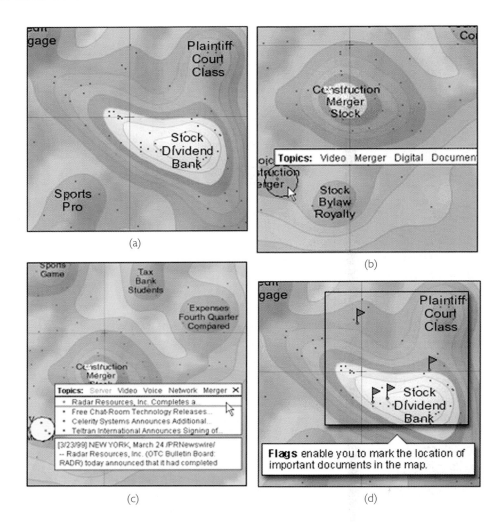

(a)

(b)

(c)

(d)

steps related to a fixed database structure. Indeed, there is no predetermined data structure: rather, a network of 'symbols' (for example, keywords, event times, locations, actions) is built up having inter-symbol weights proportional to the number of documents in which two symbols occur. On the basis of this network, symbols are sorted spatially: those closely related are positioned close to each other in a space. The location of symbols in two of the three dimensions of three-dimensional space is determined by this proximity relationship, with depth ('away' from the user) offering progressively more detail. The user's trajectory in the space, controlled by zooming, determines what appears in the user's view. As Card *et al.* (1999) remark, 'By using *time*, Galaxy of News does not need to choose a single topic for an article and the user does not need to guess which topic was used to describe an article'.

Figure 10.10 shows successive views presented to a user who first has a wide-angle view (a) of news space, chooses to investigate the Media cluster (b) and then zoom in (c) to this cluster (the word 'obituary' has appeared close to the keyword 'Media' in view of an article about the death of a comic book artist).

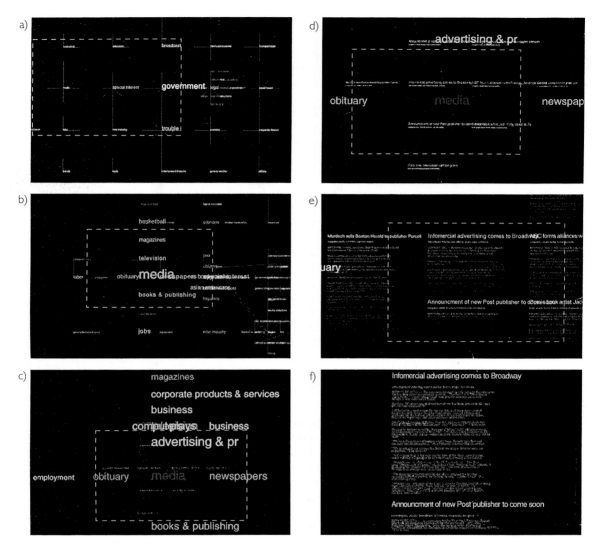

FIGURE 10.10

Successive views presented to a user of the Galaxy of News system

Source: *Rennison (1994). Rennison © 1994 Association for Computing Machinery, Inc. Reprinted by permission*

Headlines are beginning to show: finally the user sees a full presentation of an article (f). In all these six views a dashed rectangle indicates the area zoomed into to produce the following view. The user moves smoothly and immersively as they explore news space.

The Galaxy of News tool is a good example of the importance of good *visual* design, an area of expertise not always in evidence in displays designed by someone from a scientific background. Here, for example, keyword fonts are automatically adjusted with movement through space. The transparency of a keyword is carefully adjusted to facilitate movement. The colour of an article is adjusted as it moves between keyword groups. And the transparency of lines between parent and child keywords, and between keywords and articles, is adjusted appropriately.

An issue posed by the approach embodied in Galaxy of News concerns the user's internal model (see Chapter 6) of news space: a model which may not be sought if the user is purely browsing, but which is central to the activity of navigation: this issue arises because the user's view is constructed according to their movement in space. As Rennison remarks, ' . . . if a user wants to conduct a more directed search with a specific type of information in mind, then it would be useful to have personalised views or structures to assist users with navigation'.

10.5.4 Kohonen maps

Document visualization can also be based on neural network principles (Kohonen, 1990; Lin, 1997). Kohonen' self-organizing feature map algorithm (SOM) takes a set of input objects (in the example which follows they will be documents), each represented by an N-dimensional vector of 'features' (in the same example, keywords taken from titles and abstracts), and maps them onto the nodes of a two-dimensional grid. A significant feature of such a display is the 'region' in which several grid nodes reside if their response patterns to the input data are similar; such regions are arranged to be close to each other if their data are highly correlated.

The example shown in Figure 10.11 refers to 1287 documents found in DIALOG's INSPEC database as a result of the query 'Kohonen'. The 637 words that occur most often in the titles and abstracts of these documents were then used as 'features' to index the documents. The output of the process is presented on a 14 by 14 grid.

The result of applying Kohonen's algorithm reveals the main contents of the document set. The red labels on the map highlight major areas related to the topic of Kohonen mapping. For example, 'unsupervised', 'topology preserving', and 'convergence' are major characteristics of self-organizing maps. Another group comprises techniques to which SOM is often compared, including 'back propagation', 'Fuzzy Logic' and 'genetic algorithms'. Yet another group contains major application areas of SOM, examples of which are 'data visualization' and 'pattern recognition'.

The value of a Kohonen map such as the one shown in Figure 10.11 is manyfold. First, it provides a global view of the document collection, but with sufficient content to permit browsing, the creation of an internal model and then navigation to focus on whichever small area(s) appear to be of interest. The user can click on a dot to see the corresponding title or drag an area to see a list of titles in the area.

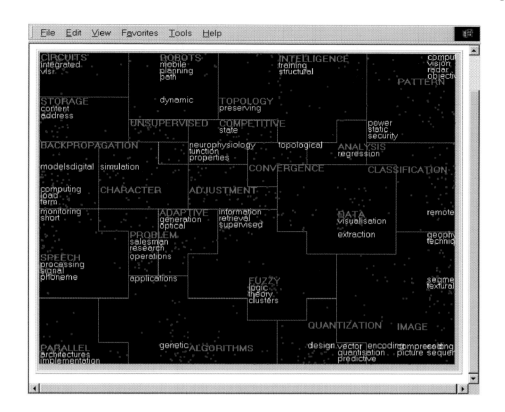

FIGURE 10.11
A Kohonen map representation of a collection of documents

Source: *Xia Lin*

References

Ahlberg, C. and Shneiderman, B. (1994) The Alphaslider: a compact and rapid selector, ACM, *Proceedings CHI '94*, pp. 365–371.

Ahlberg, C. (1996) Dynamic Queries, PhD dissertation, Chalmers University of Technology, Sweden.

Alpern, B. and Carter, L. (1991) Hyperbox, IEEE, *Proceedings Visualisation '91*, pp. 133–139.

Anstis, S.M. (1974) A chart demonstrating variations in acuity with retinal position, *Vision Research*, 14, pp. 579–582.

Apperley, M.D., Spencer, R. and Gutwin, C. (2000) *The Neighbourhood Explorer*, Working Paper 00/3, February 2000, Department of Computer Science, University of Waikato, New Zealand.

Arnold, C.J. (1997) *An Archaeology of the Early Anglo-Saxon Kingdoms*, London, Routledge, p. 216.

Baeza-Yates, R. and Ribeiro-Neto, B. (1999) *Modern Information Retrieval*, Harlow, England, Addison-Wesley.

Barber, P. and Board, C. (1993) *Tales from the Map Room*, London, BBC Books.

Barnard, P. (1991) The contributions of applied psychology to the study of human–computer interaction, in *Human Factors for Informatics Usability*, B. Shackel and S. Richardson (eds), Cambridge, UK, Cambridge University Press.

Becker, R.A. and Chambers, J.M. (1984) *An interactive Environment for Data Analysis and Graphics*, New York, Chapman and Hall.

Becker, R.A., Eick, S.G. and Wilks, A.R. (1995) Visualizing Network Data, IEEE, *Trans. on Visualization and Computer Graphics*, 1, pp.16–28.

Bederson, B.B. and Hollan, J.D. (1994) Pad++: A Zooming Graphical Interface for Exploring Alternate Interface Physics, ACM, *Proceedings UIST '94*, pp. 17–26.

Bertin, J. (1981) *Graphics and Graphic Information Processing*, Berlin, Walter de Gruyter, being a translation of Bertin, J. (1977) *La Graphique et le Traitement Graphique de l'Information*, Paris, Flammarion.

Biderman, A. (1990) The Playfair enigma: the development of the schematic representation of statistics, *Information Design Journal*, 6, 1. pp. 3–25.

Bjork, S., Holmquist, L.E. and Redstrom, J. (1999a) A Framework for Focus+Context Visualization, IEEE, *Proceedings Information Visualization '99*, pp. 53–56.

Bjork, S., Holmquist, L.E., Redstrom, J., Bretan, I., Danielson, R., Karlgren, J. and Franzen, K. (1999b) WEST: A Web Browser for Small Terminals, ACM, *Proceedings UIST '99*.

Black, F. and Scholes, M. (1973) The pricing of options and corporate liabilities, *Journal of Political Economy*, 81, pp. 637–659.

Boardman, R. (1995) Visualisation of Information Trees, Report, Department of Computing, Imperial College, London.

Boardman, R. (2000) Bubble Trees: the Visualization of Hierarchical Information Structures, ACM, Extended Abstracts, CHI 2000, pp. 315–316.

Bolt, R.A. (1979) *Spatial Data-Management*, Massachusetts Institute of Technology.

Bolt, R.A. (1984) *The Human Interface*, Belmont, C.A., Lifetime Learning Publications, p. 2.

Bondy, J.A. and Murthy, U.S.R. (1976) *Graph Theory with Applications*, London, Macmillan Press.

Borgman, C.L. (1986) Why are online catalogues hard to use? Lessons learned from information retrieval studies, *Journal of the American Society for Information Science*, 37, 6, pp. 387–400.

Bouma, H. (1970) Interaction effects in parafoveal letter recognition, *Nature*, 226, pp. 177–178.

Box, G.E.P and Draper, N.R. (1987) *Empirical Model-Building and Response Surfaces*, New York, NY, Wiley.

Boyle, G.R., Cohn, B.R., Pederson, D.O. and Solomon, J.E. (1994) Macro-modelling of integrated circuit operational amplifiers, IEEE, *J. Solid-State Circuits*, 9, pp. 353–363.

Bray, T. (1996) Measuring the Web, *Computer Networks and ISDN Systems*, 28, p. 992.

Brown, M.H. and Najork, M.A. (1998) Algorithm Animation Using Interactive 3D Graphics, in *Software Visualization*, J. Stasko *et al.* (eds), Cambridge, MA, MIT Press.

Bryson, W. (1998) *Notes from a Small Island*, London, Black Swan.

Card, S.K., Mackinlay, J.D. and Shneiderman, B. (1999) *Readings in Information Visualization*, San Francisco, CA, Morgan Kaufman.

Carmel, E., Crawford, S. and Chen, H. (1992) Browsing in Hypertext: a cognitive study, IEEE, *Transactions on Systems, Man and Cybernetics*, 22, 5, pp. 865–884.

Chalmers, M. (1993) Using a Landscape Metaphor to Represent a Corpus of Documents, in 'Spatial Information Theory – a Theoretical Basis for GIS',

Proceedings of the European Conference COSIT '93, Springer-Verlag, Lecture Notes in Computer Science, pp. 377–388.

Chalmers, M., Ingram, R. and Pfranger, C. (1996) Adding Imageability Features to Information Displays, ACM, *Proceedings of UIST '96*, pp. 33–39.

Chernoff, H. (1973) The Use of Faces to Represent Points in *k*-dimensional Space Graphically, *Journal of the American Statistical Association,* 68, pp. 361–368.

Chuah, M.C., Roth, S.F., Mattis, J. and Kolojejchick, J. (1995) SDM: Selective Dynamic Manipulation of Visualisations, ACM, *Proceedings, Symposium on User Interface Software and Technology UIST '95*, pp. 61–70.

Cleveland, W.S. (1985) *The Elements of Graphing Data,* Monterey, CA, Wadsworth Advanced Books and Software.

Cleveland, W.S. (1993) *Visualizing Data*, Summit, NJ, Hobart Press.

Cleveland, W.S. (1994) *The Elements of Graphing Data* (revised edition), Summit, NJ, Hobart Press.

Cleveland, W.S. and McGill, R. (1984) Graphical Perception: Theory, experimentation and application to the development of graphical methods, *Journal of the American Statistical Association,* 79, 387, pp. 531–554.

Cleveland, W.S. and McGill, M.E. (eds) (1988) *Dynamic Graphics for Statistics,* Pacific Grove, CA, Wadsworth & Brooks/Cole.

Colby, G. and Scholl, L. (1991) Transparency and Blur as Selective Cues for Complex Visual Information, SPIE Conference, March 1991.

Colgan, L., Spence, R. and Rankin, P.R. (1995) The Cockpit Metaphor, *Behaviour and Information Technology,* 14, 4, pp. 251–263.

Connolly, R.J. (1998) Netmap as a Visualisation Tool for Social Interaction, Living Memory/ESPRIT/i3/25621 Project, Document number LIMM/IC/RJC/98014.

Cooke, A. (1973) *Alistair Cooke's America*, London, British Broadcasting Corporation.

Davenport, E. and Buckner, K. (1998) SO-grams: a personalisation toolkit for intranet users, in *Knowledge Management and Komunicationssystem, Proceedings des 6 Internationalen Symposiums für Informationswissenschaft (ISI '98)*, H.H. Zimmermann and V. Schramm (eds), Prague, November 1998, Konstanz, Universitatsverlag Konstanz GmbH.

Davenport, E., Buckner, K. and Barr, K. (1998) SO-grams: Work-in-progress on a simple conversational prop for navigating social space, Swedish Institute of Computer Science, Technical Rept. T98:02, pp. 45–54.

Davidson, C. (1993) What your database hides away, *New Scientist*, January 9, 1993, pp. 28–31.

Dawson, R.J.McG. (1995) The 'Unusual Episode' Data Revisited, *Journal of Statistics Education*, 3, 3 (on-line).

De Bruijn, O. and Spence, R. (1999) *Rapid Serial Visual Presentation,* Video Production 1401, Imperial College Television Studio, London, Imperial College.

De Bruijn, O. and Spence, R. (2000) Rapid Serial Vision Presentation: a space–time trade-off in information presentation, *Proc. AVI 2000* pp. 189–192.

De Soete, G. (1986) A perceptual study of the Flury–Riedwyl faces for graphically displaying multivariate data, *International Journal of Man–Machine Studies,* 25, pp. 549–555.

Eick, S.G. and Wills, G.J. (1993) Navigating Large Networks with Hierarchies, IEEE, *Proceedings Information Visualization '93,* pp. 204–210.

Eick, S.G. (1994) Data Visualisation Sliders, ACM, *Proceedings of the Symposium on User Interface Technology and Software,* pp.119–120.

Eick, S.G., Steffen, J.L. and Sumner, E.E. (1992) Seesoft – A Tool for Visualizing Line Oriented Software Statistics, IEEE, *Transactions on Software Engineering,* 18, pp. 957–968.

Field, G.E. and Apperley, M.D. (1990) Context and Selective Retreat in Hierarchical Menu Structures, *Behaviour and Information Technology,* 9, 2, pp. 133–146.

Fisherkeller, M.A., Friedman, J.H. and Tukey, J.W. (1974) An interactive multidimensional data display and analysis system, SLAC PUB 1408, Stanford, CA, Stanford Linear Accelerator Center.

Flury, B. and Riedwyl, H. (1981) Graphical Representation of Multi-Variate Data by Means of Asymmetrical Faces, *Journal of the American Statistical Association,* 76, pp. 757–765.

Friendly, M. (1994) Mosaic Displays for Multi-Way Contingency Tables, *Journal of the American Statistical Association (Theory and Methods),* 89, 425, pp. 190–200.

Fua, Y-H., Ward, M. and Rudensteiner, E. (1999) Navigating Hierarchies with Structure-Based Brushes, IEEE, *Proceedings of Information Visualization '99,* pp. 58–64.

Furnas, G.W. (1981) *The FISHEYE View: A New Look at Structured Files,* Murray Hill, NJ: AT&T Bell Laboratories.

Furnas, G.W. (1986) Generalized Fisheye Views: Visualizing Complex Information Spaces, ACM, *Proc. CHI '86,* pp. 16–23.

Furnas, G.W. (1997) Effective View Navigation, ACM, *Proceedings CHI '97,* pp. 367–374.

Furnas, G.W. and Bederson, B.B. (1995) Space–Scale Diagrams: Understanding Multi-Scale Interfaces, ACM, Proc. *CHI '95,* pp. 234–241.

Furnas, G.W. and Buja, A. (1994) Prosection Views: Dimensional Inference through sections and projections, *Journal of Computational and Graphic Statistics,* 3, 4, pp. 323–353.

Furnas, G.W. and Zachs, J. (1994) Multi-trees: Enriching and reusing Hierarchical Structures, ACM, *Proceedings CHI '94,* pp. 330–336.

Furnas, G.W., Landauer, T.K., Gomez, L.M. and Dumais, S.T. (1983) Statistical Semantics: Analysis of the Potential Performance of Key-word Information Systems, *Bell System Technical Journal,* pp. 1753–1806.

Garland, K. (1994) *Mr. Beck's Underground Map: a history,* Harrow Weald, Capital Transport Publishing.

Gibson, I.E. (1997) *Theories of Visual Perception* (second edition), Chicester, Wiley.

Grinstein, G. (1999) Personal communication.

Hartigan, J.A. and Kleiner, B. (1981) Mosaics for Contingency Tables, *Computer Science and Statistics: Proceedings of the 13th Symposium on the Interface,* W.F. Eddy (ed.), New York, Springer-Verlag, pp. 268–273.

Hartigan, J.A. and Kleiner, B. (1984) A Mosaic of Television Ratings, *The American Statistician,* 38, pp. 32–35.

Hearst, M.A. (1995) TileBars: Visualisation of Term Distribution Information in Full Text Information Access, ACM, *Proceedings CHI '95*, pp. 59–66.

Hearst, M. (1999) User Interfaces and Visualization, in *Modern Information Retrieval,* R. Baeza-Yates and B. Ribeiro-Neto (eds), Harlow, England, Addison-Wesley.

Hendley, R.J., Drew, A.J., Wood, A.M. and Beale, R. (1995) Narcissus: Visualising Information, IEEE, *Proceedings Information Visualisation '95*, pp. 90–96.

Herot, C.F. (1980) Spatial Management of Data, ACM, *Transactions on Database Systems,* 5, 4, pp. 493–514.

Herot, C.F., Carling, R., Friedell, M., Kramlich, D. and Rosenberg, R.L. (1981) Overview of the Spatial Data Management System, Tech. Rept. CCA-81-08, November 1981, Computer Corporation of America.

Holmquist, L.E. (1997) Focus+Context Visualization with Flip Zooming and Zoom Browser, Exhibit, CHI '97.

Humphreys, G.W. and Bruce, V. (1989) *Visual Cognition: computational, experimental and neuropsychological perspectives,* London, LEA.

Imperial College Television Studio (1980) Focus on Information: The Office of the Professional (Video) Production No. 1003.

Inselberg, A. (1985) The Plane with Parallel Coordinates, *The Visual Computer*, 1, pp. 69–91.

Inselberg, A. (1998) Multidimensional Detective, IEEE, *Proceedings of Information Visualization '97*, pp. 100–107.

Inselberg, A. and Avidan, T. (1999) The Automated Multidimensional Detective, IEEE, *Proceedings of Information Visualization '99*, pp. 112–119.

Jackson, R., MacDonald, L. and Freeman, K. (1994) *Computer Generated Colour: A Practical Guide to Presentation and Display,* Chichester, Wiley.

Johnson, B. (1993) Treemaps: visualising hierarchical and categorical data, University of Maryland, unpublished PhD thesis.

Johnson, B. and Shneiderman, B. (1991) Tree-maps: a space-filling approach to the visualisation of hierarchical information structures, IEEE, *Proceedings Information Visualization '91,* pp. 284–291.

Kadmon, N. and Shlomi, E. (1978) A polyfocal projection for statistical surfaces, *The Cartographic Journal*, 15, 1, pp. 36–41.

Keim, D.A, Kreigel, H-P. and Seidl, T. (1993) Visual Feedback in Querying Large Databases, IEEE, *Proceedings of Visualisation '93*, pp. 158–165 and color plate CP-15.

Kohonen, T. (1990) The self-organizing map, *Proceedings IEEE*, 78, 9, pp. 1464–1480.

Koskinen, T. and Cheung, P.Y.K. (1996) Hierarchical tolerance analysis using statistical behavioural models, IEEE, *Transactions on Computer-Aided Design,* 15, pp. 506–516.

Kruskal, J.B. and Wish, M. (1979) *Multidimensional Scaling,* Newbury Park, CA, Sage Publications.

Lam, K. and Spence, R. (1997) Image Browsing – a space–time trade-off, *Proceedings INTERACT '97*, pp. 611–612.

Lamping, J. and Rao, R. (1994) Laying Out and Visualising Large Trees Using a Hyperbolic Space, ACM, *Proc. UIST '94*, pp. 13–14.

Lamping, J. and Rao, R. (1996) The Hyperbolic Browser: A Focus+Context Technique Based on Hyperbolic Geometry for Visualising Large Hierarchies, *Journal of Visual Languages and Computing*, 7, 1, pp. 33–55.

Lamping, J., Rao, R. and Pirolli, P. (1995) A Focus+Context technique based on Hyperbolic Geometry for Visualizing Large Hierarchies, ACM, *Proc. CHI '95*, pp. 401–408.

Lieberman, H. (1994) Powers of Ten Thousand, ACM, Proc. *Symposium on User Interface Software Technology*, pp. 15–16

Lieberman, H. (1997) A Multiscale, Multilayer, Translucent Virtual Space, IEEE, *Proceedings of Information Visualisation '97*, London, 27–29 August 1997, pp. 124–131.

Linx (1997) Map displays for information retrieval, *Journal of the American Society for Information Science*, 48, 1, pp. 40–54.

MacEachren, A.K., Boscoe, F.P., Haug, D. and Pickle, L. (1998) Geographic Visualisation: Designing Manipulable Maps for Exploring Temporally Varying Georeferenced Statistics, IEEE, *Proceedings Information Visualisation '98*, pp. 87–94.

MacEachren, A.M. (1995) *How Maps Work, Representation, Visualization and Design*, New York, The Guildford Press.

Mackinlay, J. (1986) Automating the design of graphical presentations, ACM *Transactions on Graphics*, 5, 2, pp. 110–141.

Mackinlay, J.D., Robertson, G.G. and Card, S.K. (1991) Perspective Wall: detail and context smoothly integrated, ACM, *Proceedings CHI '91*, pp. 173–179.

Maclean, N. (1992) *Young Men and Fire*, Chicago, University of Chicago Press.

Malone, T.W. (1983) How do people organise their desks? Implications for the design of office information systems, ACM, *Transactions on Office Information Systems*, 1, pp. 99–112.

Mendelzon, A.O. (1996) Visualizing the World Wide Web, ACM, *Proceedings AVI '96*, pp. 13–19.

Miller, G.A. (1956) The magical number seven, plus or minus two: Some limits on our capacity for processing information, *Psychological Science*, 63, pp. 81–97.

Mitta, D.A. (1990) A Fisheye Presentation Strategy: Aircraft Maintenance Data, in *Human–Computer Interaction – INTERACT '90*, Diaper, D., Gilmore, D., Cockton, G. and Shackel, B. (eds), Elsevier, pp. 875–878.

Nightingale, F. (1858) *Notes on Matters Affecting the Health, Efficiency and Hospital Administration of the British Army*, London, Harrison and Sons.

Norman, D. (1983) Some Observations on Mental Models, in *Mental Models*, D. Gentner and A.L. Stevens (eds), Hillsdale, Lawrence Erlbaum, pp. 7–14.

Norman, D. (1988) *The Psychology of Everyday Things*, New York, Basic Books, pp. 87–92.

Norman, K. (1991) *The Psychology of Menu Selection: Designing Cognitive Control at the Human/Computer Interface*, Norwood, NJ, Ablex.

Osada, M., Liao, H. and Shneiderman, B. (1993) Alphaslider: development and evaluation of text retrieval method using sliders, *Proc. 9th Symposium on Human Interface (Kobe, Japan)* pp. 91–94.

Peterson, L.R. and Peterson, M.J. (1959) Short-term retention of individual verbal items, *Journal of Experimental Psychology*, 58, pp. 193–198.

Pirolli, P. (1997) Computational Models of Information Scent-Following in a Very Large Browsable Text Collection, ACM, *Proceedings CHI '97*, pp. 3–10.

Rankin, P.R., van Heerden, C., Mama, J., Nikolovska, L., Otter, R. and Rutgers, J. (1998) Starcursors in ContentSpace, ACM, *Proceedings SIGGRAPH '98*, p. 250.

Rao, R. and Card, S.K. (1994) The Table Lens: Merging graphical and symbolic representations in an interactive focus+context visualisation for tabular information, ACM, *Proceedings CHI '94*, pp. 318–322.

Rennison, E. (1994) Galaxy of News: An Approach to Visualizing and Understanding Expansive News Landscapes, ACM, *Proceedings of Symposium on User Interface Software and Technology 1994*, pp. 3–12.

Robertson, G.G. and Mackinlay, J.D. (1993) The Document Lens, ACM, *Proceedings, 1993 Symposium on User Interface Software and Technology*, pp. 101–108.

Robertson, G.G., Mackinlay, J.D. and Card, S,K. (1991) Cone Trees: Animated 3D Visualisations of Hierarchical Information, ACM, *Proceedings of CHI '91*, pp. 189–194.

Russell, B. (1922) Preface to Wittgenstein, L. (1922) *Logisch-philosophische Abhandlung*, London, Routledge & Kegan Paul.

Salton, G., Allan, J., Buckley, C. and Singhal, A. (1995) Automatic Analysis, Theme Generation and Summarization of Machine-Readable Text, *Science*, 264, pp. 1421–1426.

Shneiderman, B. (1992) Tree Visualisation with Treemaps: A 2-dimensional Space Filling Approach, ACM, *Transactions on Graphics*, 11, 1, pp. 92–99.

Smith, D. (1999) *The State of the World Atlas*, 6th edition, London, Penguin.

Snee, R.D. (1974) Graphical Display of Two-Way Contingency Tables, *The American Statistician*, 28, pp. 9–12.

Snowberry, K., Parkinson, R. and Sisson, N. (1985) Effects of help fields on navigating through hierarchical menu structure, *International Journal of Man–Machine Studies*, 22, p. 479.

Solso, R.L. (1998) *Cognitive Psychology* (fifth edition), Boston, Allyn and Bacon.

Spence, R. (1993) A Taxonomy of Graphical Presentation, ACM, *INTERCHI '93 Adjunct Proceedings*, pp. 113–114.

Spence, R. (1996) Visualisation really has nothing to do with computers, *Proceedings Eurographics UK 1996*, pp. 1–8.

Spence, R. (1999) The Facilitation of Insight for Analog Design, IEEE, *Trans. Circuits & Systems II*, 46, 5, pp. 540–548.

Spence, R. (1999) A Framework for Navigation, *International Journal of Human–Computer Studies*, 51, 5, pp. 919–945.

Spence, R. and Apperley, M.D. (1977) The interactive man–computer dialogue in computer-aided electrical circuit design, IEEE, *Transactions on Circuits and Systems*, CAS-24, 2, pp. 49–61.

Spence, R. and Apperley, M.D. (1982) Data Base Navigation: An office environment for the professional, *Behaviour and Information Technology*, 1, 1, pp. 43–54.

Spence, R. and Drew, A. (1971) Graphical exploration in electrical circuit design and modelling, NRC, Ottawa, *Proceedings 2nd Man–Computer Communication Seminar*, pp. 61–70.

Spence, R. and Parr, M. (1991) Cognitive Assessment of Alternatives, *Interacting with Computers*, 3, 3, pp. 270–282.

Spence, R. and Soin, R.S. (1988) Tolerance Design of Electronic Circuits, London, Addison-Wesley. Also (1997), London, Imperial College Press.

Spence, R. and Tweedie, L. (1998) The Attribute Explorer: information synthesis via exploration, *Interacting with Computers*, 11, pp. 137–146.

Spoerri, A. (1993) InfoCrystal: a visual tool for information retrieval, IEEE, *Proceedings Visualisation '93*, pp. 150–157.

Stasko, J., Domingue, J., Brown, M.H. and Price, B.A. (1998) Software Visualization, Cambridge, Mass., MIT Press.

Stock, D. and Watson, C.J. (1984) Human Judgement Accuracy, Multidimensional Graphics and Humans versus Models, *Journal of Accounting Research,* 22, 1, pp. 192–206.

Stone, M., Fishkin, K. and Bier, E. (1994) The Movable Filter as a User Interface Tool, ACM, *Proceedings CHI '94,* pp. 306–312.

Su, H., Nelder, J., Wolbert, P. and Spence, R. (1996) Application of Generalised Linear Models to the Design Improvement of an Engineering Artefact, *Quality and Reliability Engineering International,* 12, pp. 101–112.

Suchman, L.A. (1987) *Plans and Situated Actions*, Cambridge, Cambridge University Press.

Tauscher, L.A. and Greenberg, S. (1997) Revisitation: Patterns in World Wide Web Navigation, ACM, *Proceedings CHI '97*, pp. 399–406.

Tufte, E. (1983) *The Visual Display of Quantitative Information*, Cheshire, CT, Graphics Press.

Tufte, E.R. (1990) *Envisioning Information*, Cheshire, CT, Graphics Press.

Tufte, E.R. (1997) *Visual Explanations*, Cheshire, CT, Graphics Press.

Tversky, B. (1993) Cognitive Maps, Cognitive Collages and Spatial Mental Models, in 'Spatial Information Theory – a Theoretical Basis for GIS', *Proceedings of the European Conference COSIT '93*, Springer-Verlag, Lecture Notes in Computer Science, pp. 14–24.

Tweedie, L. (1995) Interactive Visualisation Artifacts: how can abstractions inform design? in *People and Computers X, Proceedings of HCI '95,* pp. 247–265.

Tweedie, L. (1997) Exploiting Interactivity in Graphical Problem Solving: from visual cues to insight, London University, PhD Thesis.

Tweedie, L., Smith, A., Malik, Z. and Spence, R. (1998) Contextual Model Fitting, IEEE, *Proceedings Information Visualisation '98* (late breaking papers) pp. 25–27.

Tweedie, L. and Spence, R. (1998) The Prosection Matrix: A tool to support the interactive exploration of statistical models and data, *Computational Statistics,* 13, pp. 65–76.

Tweedie, L., Spence, R., Dawkes, H. and Su, H. (1995) The Influence Explorer, ACM, *Companion Proceedings CHI '95,* pp. 129–130.

Tweedie, L., Spence, R., Dawkes, H. and Su, H. (1996) Externalising Abstract Mathematical Models, ACM, *Proceedings CHI '96,* pp. 406–412.

Tweedie, L., Spence, R., Williams, D. and Bhogal, R. (1994) The Attribute Explorer, ACM, *Video Proceedings CHI '94.*

Unwin, A.R., Hawkins, G., Hofmann, H. and Siegl, B. (1996) 'Interactive Graphics for Data Sets with Missing Values', MANET, *Journal of Computational and Graphical Statistics*, 5, 2, pp. 113–122.

Unwin, A.R. (1999) Requirements for interactive graphics software for exploratory data analysis, Computational Statistics, 14, pp. 7–22.

Viegas, F.B. and Donath, J.S. (1999) Chat Circles, ACM, *Proceedings CHI '99,* pp. 9–16.

Wainer, H. (1997) *Visual Revelations*, New York, Copernicus Springer-Verlag.

Ware, C. (2000) *Information Visualization: Perception for Design*, San Francisco, CA, Morgan Kaufmann.

Ware, C. and Lewis, M. (1995) The DragMag Image Magnifier, *Video Program and Companion Proceedings CHI '95*, pp. 407–408.

Waugh, N.C. and Norman, D.A. (1965) Primary Memory, *Psychological Review, 72,* pp. 89–104.

Wegman, E.J. (1990) Hyperdimensional Data Analysis Using Parallel Coordinates, *Journal of the American Statistical Association,* 85, 411, Theory and Methods, pp. 664–675.

Westphal, C. and Blaxton, T. (1998) *Data Mining Solutions*, New York, Wiley.

Wexelblat, A. and Maes, P. (1999) Footprints: History-Rich Tools for Information Foraging, ACM, *Proceedings CHI '99*, pp. 270–277.

Williamson, C. and Shneiderman, B. (1992) The Dynamic Homefinder: evaluating dynamic queries in a real estate information exploration system, ACM, *Proceedings SIGIR '92,* pp. 339–346.

Wise, J.A., Thoma, J.J., Pennock, K., Lantrip, D., Pottier, M., Schur, A. and Crow, V. (1995) Visualising the Non-Visual: Spatial Analysis and Interaction with Information from Text Documents, IEEE, *Proceedings of InfoViz '95,* pp. 51–58.

Wittenburg, K, Ali-Ahmad, W., LaLiberte, D. and Lanning, T. (1998) Rapid-Fire Image Previews for Information Navigation, ACM, *Proceedings AVI '98,* pp. 76–82.

Yamaashi, K., Tani, M. and Tanikoski, K. (1993) Fisheye Videos: Distorting Multiple Videos in Space and Time Domain according to Users' Interests, ACM, *INTERCHI '93 Adjunct Proceedings,* pp. 119–120.

York, J. and Bohn, S. (1995) Clustering and Dimensionality Reduction in SPIRE. Presented at the Automated Intelligence Processing and Analysis Symposium, Tysons Corner, VA, March 28–30, 1995.

Index